LITTLE FARM DOWN THE LANE
BOOK VII

"Saying Good-bye"

by

Bonnie Bedi Siegrist

Blessings!

xulon PRESS

Bonnie Bedi Siegrist

Little Farm Down the Lane—Book VII
by Bonnie Bedi Siegrist

Printed in the United States of America

ISBN 9781619042339

Unless otherwise indicated, Bible quotations are taken from the King James Version of the Bible.

Cover picture by Steven T. Flanagan

Drawings designed by Sarah L Bedi

www.xulonpress.com

CONTENTS

Chapter 1

THERE'S NO PLACE LIKE HOME

Bonnie couldn't believe it! Mommy wanted to move!
She sighed unhappily and fidgeted on the hard pew, trying to find a more comfortable position. She'd been eagerly awaiting this much-talked-about series on Africa. Now, although the first meeting was about to start, her mind was not on Africa, but on the disturbing statement her mother had made at the supper table an hour earlier—she wanted to leave the farm!

From the time they had moved to the Snyder farm when she was a young child, Bonnie had known Mommy was not as happy there as she and Daddy were, but she had never even considered the possibility of living anywhere else.

She glanced at Paula, sitting next to her. Her curly blond head was bent over the book Mommy had given her to keep her occupied. Bonnie remembered the way she and her parents had celebrated when Paula was born, over five-and-a-half-years-ago on the very first anniversary of their moving to the farm, followed in quick succession by two little boys.

Daddy, strong and handsome, sat beside Paula, his arm resting on the pew behind her. Three-and-a-half-year-old Billy, his chubby little face surrounded by dark hair slicked back with Vaseline, sat on the opposite side of him. Mommy, looking stylish and pretty, as usual, sat next to Billy, holding Tommy on her lap. He had already turned two, but was still so adorable they continued to refer to him as "baby Tommy."

We're the perfect family to live on a farm, Bonnie told herself. *Two strong healthy adults to do the housework and the farm work, plus two girls to help Mommy and two boys to*

1

grow up and help Daddy. After all, hadn't Daddy beamed with pride and said those very words after Tommy was born?

Yes! We're perfect for the farm! Bonnie concluded again. *We just can't move!* She shook her head vigorously at the very idea of it. Embarrassed, she glanced around to see if anyone noticed. Thankfully, no one had.

"Everyone please stand." Reverend Mark's voice cut in on her fretful musings. "Let's open our Annual Missionary Conference this year by singing hymn number thirty-two."

Bonnie found the page and shared the hymnbook with Paula. Paula couldn't read yet, but she liked to pretend she could. They both loved to sing, and soon they were belting out the familiar words of "Go Tell It on the Mountain." The people around them smiled at their enthusiasm. Bonnie didn't care. Her favorite part of any service was the music. She and Paula would sing as loudly as they wanted to sing!

As the song ended, a dark-haired, young woman marched briskly down the aisle to the front of the church, carrying a large piece of cardboard that completely hid her trim figure.

"As you know," Miss Hartenstine reminded the congregation, "I've been accepted by the mission board. I will be leaving for Africa sometime next year. In the meantime, there's something we here at the Evangelical United Brethren Church of Neffsville, Pennsylvania, can do to help the missionaries already toiling away in Africa."

She placed the cardboard on an easel in front of the pulpit. On it was a large thermometer. Inside it were numbered lines. Starting at ten, the numbers went up—ten, twenty, thirty…all the way to one hundred at the top. Miss Hartenstine explained that the numbers stood for dollars. "Each night we will fill in the amount of money received in red. If everyone brings an offering each night this week, I know we can reach our goal of one hundred dollars toward purchasing *this* for our African missionaries." With a flourish, she grabbed a poster hidden behind the pulpit and held it up. It was a picture of a brand-new red Chevy truck. Bonnie, along with everyone around her, gasped in pleasant surprise.

Miss Hartenstine reached behind the pulpit a second time and brought out two buckets. "And to make it more exciting, there will be a contest between the men and the women." She placed a bucket on each side of the pulpit. One was marked BOYS. One was marked GIRLS.

Miss Hartenstine waited for the clapping and cheering to subside before going on. "Whichever group brings in the most offering by the end of the week will earn a small prize for each person in their group. Dig deep into your pockets, folks!" she continued passionately. "Give sacrificially! Let's make our goal!" She invited all those who brought an offering to come up and put it in the appropriate bucket.

As people headed to the front of the church, Bonnie slumped down in her seat, ashamed. She had been so upset by Mommy's announcement that she had not remembered to bring an offering. Suddenly something cold touched the back of her hand. Mommy was handing her and Paula each a quarter. Overjoyed, they both bounded down the aisle and threw their coins in the girls' bucket—just in time to see Daddy and little Billy each drop a quarter into the boys' bucket. Daddy winked at Bonnie, who couldn't help smiling back. They had balanced each other out, but that was okay; at least they were helping the missionaries!

By the time Bonnie settled back into her seat, Rev. Mark was introducing the speaker. "We are honored to have with us this week John Smith, who has been a missionary to Kenya since 1947. I know before he even begins his program tonight that you will not be bored. His love for God and his dedication to His work permeates every word he speaks. His sense of humor, incredible slides, and miraculous stories will leave you spellbound. But beyond and far greater than all this,

3

I know he will instill a new determination in us to help carry the gospel of Jesus Christ to Africa in any way we can."

Rev. Mark was right. Bonnie sat on the edge of her seat every night that week. She laughed until her sides ached at Mr. Smith's hilarious jokes. Tears filled her eyes as she listened in awe to the stories of how God had saved his life, healed him of a bad case of malaria, protected him from a heathen medicine man, and provided needed supplies just when he could no longer have survived without them.

And the slides of poor, half-naked little black children, sitting in the dirt in front of makeshift grass huts—their bellies swollen with hunger, their round eyes sad and pleading—touched Bonnie somewhere deep inside.

All that week, when she arrived home from school, Bonnie, along with Paula and Billy, did as many chores as they could to earn money for the offering. After a quick supper, Bonnie washed and dried the dishes, Mommy spruced up Paula and the boys, and Daddy did the evening chores. Then they were off to church. Each night's session was better than the one before. Afterward, all the way home in the car, Bonnie pondered the things Mr. Smith had said.

The last night of the week, to Bonnie and Paula's delight and Billy's huge disappointment, the girls edged the boys out and won the prize. Bonnie, Paula, and Mommy proudly pinned the gold crosses they received to their blouses, but the best reward of all was the overflowing thermometer. The offering far exceeded everyone's expectations!

As they drove in the lane that night, Mommy added the final touch to a near-perfect week. She quoted her favorite saying, something she had not said for quite a long time.

"Be it ever so humble, there's no place like home."

Bonnie's heart leaped with joy and relief. In spite of the marvelous conference, she had not forgotten Mommy's upsetting announcement. Maybe, just maybe, Mommy had changed her mind. Maybe they would stay on the farm!

Chapter 2

A CHANGE FOR DADDY

Bonnie stepped off the school bus and shivered in the sharp wind. She buttoned up her thick sweater and tied a wool bandana over her head before starting down the gravel lane.

Gray clouds hung low over the late November sky like a thick blanket. Occasionally the sun peeked through, but its short-lived rays added little warmth to the damp, dreary day.

The crops were stored for the coming winter. The land surrounding the farm lay barren and brown, except for a tree here and there, desperately clinging to its few remaining leaves. Geese, in v-formation, flew high in the sky, cackling and calling to one another in the chilly air.

The pungent aroma of curing tobacco greeted Bonnie as she reached the s-curve in the lane. She was almost home! She picked up speed, hurrying by the tobacco shed and around the old barn. Veering left, she followed the narrow cement walk up through the yard to the waiting farmhouse.

"Brrrr. It's so good to be home!" she exclaimed a few moments later as she warmed herself by the cook stove.

"It is nice and cozy in here," Mommy agreed. She glanced up from the potatoes she was peeling and smiled at Bonnie. Lately Mommy seemed happier. Since the missionary conference, she had not mentioned moving again. Bonnie was careful not to mention it either. Things had settled into the normal fall/winter routine of school and church activities, followed by contented evenings of family time and favorite television programs. Bonnie wanted to keep it that way.

Mommy's voice broke into her thoughts. "I declare," she said, looking Bonnie up and down, "since you entered the fifth grade this fall, you've blossomed into a young lady. You're getting so tall! Where did my little girl disappear to?"

Bonnie's friends at school had noticed the same thing. She thought about their conversation as she charged up the stairs two at a time to change out of her school clothes.

Barbara, who had always been the tallest of the four best friends, said one day, "You've caught up to me!" They stood back-to-back and measured. Sure enough, it was true!

Sheila, a little on the plump side, sighed longingly. "The only way I seem to grow is out!"

Kathy consoled her. "Don't worry. I'll never be tall either. I'm the shortest person in a short family."

After Bonnie donned everyday slacks and an old blouse in the chilly upstairs, she took a moment to inspect herself in the bureau mirror. They were right. She was taller, and she did look older since she'd lost her baby fat. Inspecting her face, she decided her nose would pass, but her chin was rather pointy and her brown eyes were ordinary and small. Everyone said her dimples were her best feature. Bonnie smiled at herself, and, for an instant, the face in the mirror was transformed into something almost pretty. Shocked, Bonnie shrugged and tore off downstairs. She wasn't ready to grow up yet.

Mommy was sitting at the kitchen table, a pen in her hand. Spread out in front of her was her Bible, several books, and a tablet. She taught the women's Sunday school class and she took her job seriously, studying for hours, saying anything one did for God should be done to the best of one's ability.

Noticing Bonnie, she said, "I

want to work on this week's lesson before preparing supper. Please watch the little ones."

Obediently, Bonnie headed for the living room. The instant Paula saw her she cried out, "I'm not a baby. I can take care of myself!" Her green eyes flashed in defiance.

Mommy settled the matter from the kitchen. "Paula, you may come and sit at the table with me as long as you play quietly. Bonnie, keep an eye on the boys."

Bonnie was glad Mommy had bailed her out. Paula was becoming more independent with each passing day. She especially hated having to obey her big sister. Bonnie dreaded the times Mommy put her in charge of Paula. They always ended up arguing. Worse yet, Paula usually won.

The boys were easier to watch. They played well together and seldom fought, but Bonnie had learned the hard way not to take her eyes off them. Billy contented himself for hours with the same toy, but baby Tommy was a curious little fellow. The minute she turned her back, he was into something. Once, when Bonnie left the room for a few minutes, he went into the bathroom, discovered a box of powdered detergent, and managed to sprinkle it over most of the bathroom and living room floors before she returned. Of course, she had to help clean up the awful mess!

While her eyes must stay riveted on the boys, her thoughts were free to roam. Though several weeks had passed since the missionary conference, her mind kept returning to Mr. Smith's final challenging words. He quoted Isaiah 6:8—"*Also I heard the voice of the Lord, saying, Whom shall I send, and who will go for us? Then said I, Here am I: send me.*" Afterward, Mr. Smith asked a haunting question: "Are **you** willing to say, 'Here am I! Send me!'?"

Bonnie had wanted to be a missionary to deepest, darkest Africa ever since she could remember. On one hand, Mr. Smith's passionate cry for help set her aflame with a burning desire to answer the call with an emphatic "Yes!" On the other hand, hearing him describe all he had given up and the great difficulties he had faced, gave her a new realization of what the words "deepest, darkest Africa" truly meant.

The farmhouse might not be a mansion, but it was safe and warm. Paula might give her a hard time, and Tommy might get her into trouble, but she still cared about them, not to mention her parents, little Billy, and her friends. Mr. Smith admitted it had been four years since his last visit home. It would be another four years until he came again. Bonnie couldn't imagine leaving those she loved for such a long time.

Then there was the tropical climate—hot, humid, and miserable—the kind of weather she disliked the most. Added to that were the unsanitary conditions, death-threatening illnesses, wild animals, slimy snakes, and biting bugs.

Did she have the courage to say, "Here am I, send me"? She admitted to herself that she was glad she was not old enough yet to have to answer that question.

Mommy had finished studying, and supper was on the table by the time Daddy arrived home from work. "I'm starving, and the chicken potpie smells delicious!" he said, quickly washing up at the sink. They all sat down and automatically bowed their heads. Even baby Tommy was quiet while Daddy said the grace. Hungry, everyone dug in.

"You'd think we hadn't eaten for a week!" Mommy said.

Daddy agreed. "This family loves to eat, that's for sure!"

Bonnie and the rest of the family had devoured the potpie and were taking their first bites of Mommy's scrumptious graham cracker pudding when Daddy cleared his throat in a way that meant he had something important to say.

"As you know, Annabell," he began, sounding excited, but with a hint of reservation in his voice, "when I started at Penn Boiler and Burner, they promised to teach me to be a machinist if I did well during my six-month trial period." He paused dramatically for a moment before blurting out, "Today my boss informed me I'm in! My training starts next week."

"That's great news!" Mommy rejoiced. But a few seconds later, she asked, "What *aren't* you telling me, Bill? They are giving you the six-month raise they promised you, along with your promotion and training, right?"

"Yes, I got my raise," Daddy assured her.

"Thank the Lord!" Mommy cried out in relief. "It's small, but we sure can use it with four kids to feed and clothe."

"Yes, we can," Daddy agreed, but he sounded worried.

"There *is* something bothering you! What is it, Bill?"

"Nothing," Daddy replied, but his face said otherwise.

Mommy persisted. "What is it?"

"I'm probably worrying about nothing."

"Tell me!" Mommy insisted.

"I'll have to work my regular eight-hour shift every day, plus put in fifteen hours of extra training each week," Daddy informed her. "That means ten-hour days plus Saturday mornings for the next couple of years until I'm certified."

Mommy sighed heavily. "I'm going to mind your being gone so much. You know how lonely I get out here in the country with no car all day. But if that's what it takes for you to have a good trade that will provide well for us in the future, I'm willing to make the sacrifice. Maybe then we can get off this farm and buy a place of our own."

Although happy for Daddy, Bonnie had only been half listening to the conversation, more intent on shoveling the yummy graham cracker pudding into her mouth. At the mention of leaving the farm, however, she suddenly lost her appetite. Mommy had not forgotten about moving! She had just been biding her time. Totally alert now, Bonnie listened more carefully to the conversation between her parents.

Daddy continued. "I knew you wouldn't like my long hours," he confessed to Mommy, "but I also knew you'd understand. It's not you I'm concerned about. It's Ivan."

"Mr. Snyder?" Mommy and Bonnie said at the same time.

"Yes, Mr. Snyder," Daddy repeated. "Since I took this job, he hasn't been happy. He wants me to work nights as I used to at the asbestos factory, so I'll have more hours during the day to devote to farm work. A couple of times lately he's complained about my not pulling my weight around here. He's not going to be too happy when he finds out about this."

"He wouldn't just kick us out without any notice, would he?" Now Mommy sounded worried.

"I don't think so, but he is the owner. The agreement is that I help with the farm chores in exchange for the rent."

"You do help, Bill!" Mommy said indignantly. "You work as hard as two men! No matter how tired you are, whenever Ivan calls, you drop everything and go."

"I just hope he sees it that way," Daddy said with a sigh.

Mommy took her last bite of pudding and stood up. "So do I!" she agreed. "I want to get off this smelly farm, but we don't have nearly the money we need yet. We have to wait until you start making a machinist's pay in a few years."

Daddy stood up too. "Well, the first thing I'd better do, if we want to keep living here, is get my evening farm chores done. Don't worry, Annabell." Daddy's usual smile was back on his face. "Ivan's a reasonable man. Things will work out."

"Yes, they will!" Mommy said emphatically, "because, as of right now, I'm going to pray that God will provide the money for a house of our own someday."

As she helped clear the dishes, Bonnie cheered up. She was certain nice Mr. Ivan would never ask them to leave the farm. Besides, they didn't have the money to move! Of course, Mommy's prayers were powerful, but she was praying that *someday* they would have the money they needed. It was the same as Bonnie's becoming a missionary. *Someday* she would have to face that decision, but not now. Thankfully, *someday* was still a long time away.

Chapter 3

GREEN STAMPS

Mommy waved the grocery section of the newspaper in Daddy's face. "Look!" she complained. "Hamburger fifty-six cents a pound! Bread eighteen cents a loaf! Coffee eighty cents a pound! With these prices, even your raise won't help."

"I know what you mean," Daddy replied. "I paid twenty-three cents a gallon for gas last week!"

"At least stamps are still only three cents," Mommy said.

The boys were in bed. The rest of the family was sitting in front of the television waiting for *Father Knows Best* to come on. They had not missed an episode since it first aired that fall. Mommy and Daddy liked the good values it taught. Bonnie enjoyed watching Betty, the Andersons' pretty daughter, solve her teenage problems, and she couldn't help laughing at the mischievous antics of her younger brother Bud, while Paula's eyes were fixed on their cute little sister, whom Mr. Anderson affectionately called "Kitten."

It was nearly time for the show when Mommy spoke again. "Paula, please go to the kitchen and get everyone some of those oatmeal raisin cookies I baked this afternoon."

"Yippee!" Paula squealed with delight and hurried off.

Mommy turned to Bonnie. "I want to talk about money for Christmas. You're old enough to understand. Paula isn't."

Bonnie nodded. Mommy directed her next words to Daddy. "Christmas is only three weeks away, and I still haven't been able to save any money for presents. I've been praying about it, and I believe God has given me an answer."

"I've been worrying about it too," Daddy confessed. "If you have a solution, I'm all ears!"

Mommy said triumphantly, "We can use green stamps!"

Bonnie sighed with relief. She might be old enough to understand who pays for the gifts under the tree on Christmas morning, but she was still selfish enough to want those gifts.

"Green stamps!" Daddy echoed. "Do we have enough?"

"I've been saving them for years. I had my heart set on a new living room suite when we moved off the farm, but that isn't happening anytime soon, so why not use them now?"

Daddy wasn't sure. "You do without so many nice things already, Annabell. I hate to see you give up another dream."

Mommy shrugged it off. "I can wait."

"Well, if you're sure about this," Daddy gave in.

"I'm sure!" Mommy said determinedly. "Bonnie, after *Father Knows Best* is over and Paula is in bed, you can help us count the booklets.... Shhh! Here comes Paula."

The show was so entertaining Bonnie forgot all about the stamps. Mommy did not. She came downstairs after tucking Paula in and went straight to the bottom desk drawer.

Bonnie did not have to look inside to know it held booklets full of stamps. Whenever Mommy came home from shopping, the Bedi children loved pasting in all the stamps she brought. Mommy only shopped at stores that handed out S&H green stamps. To her, they were like money in the bank.

They started counting, their excitement mounting as the pile of booklets continued to grow. Finally, Bonnie shouted with glee, "We have thirty-nine books!"

"I had no idea there were so many!" Daddy marveled.

"I knew I'd saved a lot of stamps," Mommy said, "but even I'm shocked! Thank you, Lord! Thank you, Lord!"

After that night, Mommy and Daddy never mentioned green stamps again, but on Christmas morning, there were wonderful presents under the tree. Bonnie, Paula, and the boys were ecstatic. But looking into her parents' beaming faces, Bonnie knew they had received the best gift of all.

Chapter 4

THE WATCH

The alarm clock blared in the pre-dawn darkness. Bonnie snuggled deeper under the covers, putting off, as long as possible, the moment she had to leave the cozy nest. She dreaded getting dressed in the freezing cold bedroom.

Later, running to catch the school bus, she faced another thing she hated about winter—the long, bone-chilling trek out the lane in the icy January wind.

The warm bus was a welcome relief. Annette, a neighbor and friend since early childhood, climbed aboard at the next stop. As usual, she sat in the seat behind Bonnie and happily chattered away. "I almost froze waiting for the bus. My dad says it's in the teens this morning and there's going to be snow later this week.... Johnny Burkhart got in trouble yesterday. He had to go to the principal's office. I bet he got a paddling.... Oh, I forgot to ask you yesterday in church; can you come over Saturday morning and play? My mother says it's okay as long as we're done by noon. She has errands to run. I got lots of new toys for Christmas. Wanna come?"

Bonnie had not been to Annette's house for a while. Annette still liked dolls and tinker toys. Bonnie, two years older, had outgrown them. Still, Annette, with her happy-go-lucky attitude, was fun to be around. And among the new toys, there was sure to be something Bonnie would enjoy. Besides that, the Longs' refrigerator was always full of yummy treats, probably the reason Annette and her mom were rather on the chubby side. Best of all, though, were the tempting candy dishes sitting around, waiting to be emptied.

"Okay, I'll ask my mom if I can come," Bonnie decided.

On Friday night, it snowed, just as Annette's father predicted, and by Saturday morning, a thick layer of white covered the ground. Daddy said the roads were passable. He put chains on the car tires and left for work early. Bonnie would have to walk to Annette's later if she wanted to go.

Mommy was not keen on the idea. "It's freezing out there. Stay home or wait until it warms up a little," she advised.

"I want to go, and they're going away in the afternoon," Bonnie argued, thinking if she stayed home, she'd be stuck with the usual Saturday morning chores. "I'll be okay."

"Well, bundle up," Mommy said, giving in. "Leave at noon. I don't want you holding up Mrs. Long's schedule."

"I won't," Bonnie promised. She dressed quickly and hurried out the door before Mommy could change her mind.

By the time she reached Annette's house, she knew she should have listened to Mommy. In spite of being bundled up like a mummy, her fingers were numb, her feet were like blocks of ice, and her nose was almost frostbitten.

Mr. Long was shoveling off the front walk. He greeted her pleasantly, "Hello. We've missed your visits. Go right in."

Without knocking, Bonnie opened the kitchen door. "Come in! Come in!" Mrs. Long exclaimed. "You must be frozen stiff! Sit up. Have some hot cocoa with Annette."

The cocoa's sweet warmth slowly thawed Bonnie out. As she downed the last delicious drop, Annette, who had already finished her cocoa, demanded impatiently, "Let's go play!"

Annette was an only child, so her parents doted on her. Her playroom overflowed with every imaginable toy. Soon she and Bonnie were busy playing. It seemed like only a short time had passed when, right in the middle of a game of Parcheesi, Annette cried out, "I'm hungry!" Bonnie glanced at the clock, amazed to see it was time to go! And, now that Annette had mentioned it, she realized she was hungry too.

While Annette put the game away, Bonnie hurried to the kitchen and put on her coat. As she bent down to pull on her boots, she spied a dish of gumdrops sitting in the middle of the table. Instinctively, her hand reached out to take some, but she pulled it back. Mommy had taught her it was not polite to take candy unless it was offered. But as she put on her cap, her eyes were irresistibly drawn back to the gumdrops.

Mrs. Long was nowhere in sight, but she had always told Bonnie to feel free to help herself. Still, Bonnie hesitated. She stood there holding her mittens, undecided, staring longingly at the candy, until she could no longer resist the temptation. She reached into the bowl and grabbed a handful.

Just as she did, Mrs. Long came around the corner. Feeling a little guilty, Bonnie quickly stuffed the candy into her pocket. Just then, Annette entered the room. Late already, Bonnie slipped on her mittens, said good-bye, and left.

On the way home, Bonnie fingered the candy in her pocket, but soon she was too cold to care about anything except getting warm. At home, she stripped off her outer gear and stood behind the wrought iron cook stove in the kitchen, shivering, while Mommy put lunch on the table.

It was late afternoon before Bonnie remembered the candy and stuffed the gumdrops greedily into her mouth. They didn't taste nearly as good as she had anticipated. She wasn't sure why, but she decided next time she would wait until the candy was offered before taking any. It tasted better that way.

The next day in church, Annette was her friendly self, but her parents seemed distant. They didn't even say "hi," which puzzled Bonnie. They were usually very friendly. She shrugged it off. Maybe they weren't feeling well.

That afternoon, as Mommy stood at the sink drying dishes, she glanced out the window and exclaimed, "What in the world are the Longs doing here? We just saw them!" Frantically she scurried about, putting the last of the dishes away, shouting orders at the same time. "Bonnie, hurry up! Make sure the living room's decent. Billy, pick up your toys! Paula, check to see if the bathroom's clean."

In the time it took for the Longs to reach the kitchen door, the family managed to put the house in presentable order. "Come in. Long time, no see," Daddy jokingly welcomed them. Mr. Long barely smiled. Mrs. Long didn't smile at all, but Annette did. "Isn't this great? My parents need to talk to your parents, so we get to play together again!"

Whatever the Longs wanted to talk about must be serious from their unhappy faces, but it was the grownups' problem, not hers. Bonnie grabbed Annette's hand and led her out to the lean-to shed. She and Paula had received roller skates for Christmas, and that was something Annette did not have.

Annette had just fallen for about the fifth time when Mommy appeared at the shed door. "Bonnie, I need to speak with you!" She sounded terribly upset. Bonnie's heart skipped a beat. Was she in trouble? She followed Mommy upstairs to her bedroom. Mommy motioned for her to sit on the bed, sat down beside her, and got right to the point. "Melvin owns a watch, a valuable heirloom. It is missing. The Longs believe you stole it. Is there any truth to this?"

Bonnie was flabbergasted! How could the Longs think such a thing? She cried out in dismay, "Why would I take his watch? You gave me one for Christmas."

"That's what I said," Mommy replied. "But Anna says she saw you take it." The accusation stabbed Bonnie like a knife.

She jumped up screaming, "That's a lie! She couldn't have, because I didn't! I promised God a long time ago I would never steal, and I have kept that promise!"

"I believe you, Bonnie, Honey." Mommy's faith in her was a great comfort. However, the feelings of hurt and betrayal were so deep that she couldn't hold back the tears.

Mommy held her and waited patiently until Bonnie regained control of her emotions and then continued. "The Longs are godly people. This is not like them. Something must have happened to cause them to arrive at this awful conclusion. Can you think of anything you might have done?"

16

Bonnie shook her head. "Think, Bonnie," Mommy insisted. "There must be something!" In her mind's eye, Bonnie went back over her visit. Then it occurred to her what must have happened. She told Mommy about putting the gumdrops in her pocket just as Mrs. Long entered the room.

Mommy understood immediately. "Anna saw your guilty look and thought you were putting the watch in your pocket. Oh, Bonnie, if only you had listened to me and waited until the candy was offered, all of this could have been avoided." She sighed and went on. "What's done is done, but in the future, I hope you obey the rules of etiquette I taught you. Now go play with Annette. I'll square this with the Longs."

Mommy explained the situation to the Longs, and they said they understood. But over the following weeks, Bonnie could tell by the way they avoided her that, deep down inside, they still believed she had taken the watch. It hurt that they didn't believe her, and the pain overshadowed her life.

On the last day of January, the phone rang. Mommy listened intently to the person on the other end and then said, "I'm so happy for you. I know how much it means to you."

"Who was that?" Bonnie asked curiously, as Mommy hung up.

"You'll never believe it!" Mommy exclaimed. "Mr. Long found his watch, and it was right where he left it!"

"But you said they turned the house inside out looking for it. Why didn't they find it then?" Bonnie wanted to know.

"Because it wasn't in the house," Mommy explained. "Apparently, Melvin absent-mindedly took it off to protect it while he was shoveling snow on the morning you visited. He laid it on the porch railing. It must have fallen into a crack between the railing and the porch post. We had several snowstorms since then, which covered the crack, so the watch remained hidden. Yesterday afternoon the sun came out and the temperature went up to fifty degrees, melting the snow. When Melvin went out to feed his sheep, his eye caught the

17

reflection of something by the post. And there was his watch! And, although a little worse for wear, it still worked!"

"But why didn't he remember he'd taken it off?" Bonnie could not understand how he could possibly forget.

"I think I know the answer to that," Mommy replied. "As soon as Anna told him she saw you putting something in your pocket, he immediately assumed you took the watch. His mind was so set on what he thought was true, he didn't bother to think any further, so he forgot the real truth."

"That can happen?" It was hard for Bonnie to believe.

"Oh, yes," Mommy assured her. "We can believe a lie if we don't look hard enough for the truth."

"Well, at least I'm glad he called to apologize."

"He didn't apologize," Mommy informed her.

"What?" Bonnie cried in disbelief. "But a Christian's supposed to admit when he's wrong and ask forgiveness!"

"Yes," Mommy agreed, "but in order to do that, he has to swallow his pride and admit he was wrong. Instead, I think the Longs are justifying themselves, thinking you deserved their distrust because you looked so guilty. That way they don't have to humble themselves and apologize."

Bonnie felt her face grow hot with anger, but before she could say a word, Mommy turned toward her, looked straight into her eyes, and softly spoke again. "Now it's *your* turn to do what's right. You have to forgive *them*."

Forgiving the Longs was not easy. February came and went before Bonnie could bring herself to say "hello" to them, and the blustery winds of March had died away before she could add a smile to that "hello." As the first signs of spring appeared and the last snow melted into the ground, the final drops of her bitterness finally seeped away with it. But, it had taken the entire long, cold winter for God to heal her hurting heart.

Chapter 5

THE SPOILED DINNER

Trouble doesn't just visit in the dead of winter. It comes calling on beautiful spring days too. And on one such day in April, it decided to pay Mommy an unexpected visit.

During spring break, Bonnie's cousin Woody, who lived over an hour's drive away, came to stay overnight. He was two years younger than Bonnie was, tow-headed, and all boy, but Bonnie was still tomboyish enough to enjoy his favorite things—climbing trees and making tunnels in the hay. She showed Woody her secret hideout in the curve of the lane; he taught her how to play spy and write secret codes. They had such a good time that Woody decided he wanted to stay longer. Mommy called up Aunt Marylou to see if it was okay.

Bonnie and Woody listened anxiously to Mommy's side of the conversation. They heard her say, "Why don't you pick him up on Saturday morning and stay for lunch if you want to?" When Mommy nodded "yes" to them, they shouted with glee and hurried outside, ecstatic to have another day to play.

That evening at supper, Mommy ran an idea by Daddy. "Your sister Marylou is always feeding us. We go there three or four times a year for family gatherings since it's your dad's home too, but they rarely come here. She's such a gracious hostess and always serves us wonderful meals. For once, I'd like to return the favor. I want to make a special meal for her and her family when they come on Saturday."

Daddy liked the idea. "I'll be home from work by noon, and I don't have to help Ivan until four, so that should work."

"I have another idea," Mommy said, getting excited, now that Daddy agreed with her. "Ivan said we could have a couple of spring chickens. Tomorrow, why don't you pick out two of the best ones in the chicken house and…" She glanced at the little ones. "…uh, you know. Afterward, I'll pluck their feathers and do the rest. They'll make a delicious meal."

Bonnie lost her appetite. What Mommy was suggesting was the one thing she hated about farm life. No matter how often Daddy explained that farm animals were not pets but provided needed food, she still could not accept what happened to them. Now to her horror, Daddy was going to be the one doing the terrible deed!

Woody, however, didn't share her feelings. "Can I watch, Uncle Bill?"

Daddy looked doubtful. "It's not a very pleasant sight."

"I saw Grandpa Bedi do it once," Woody said, matter-of-factly. "They're just chickens."

"Well, okay then, but I hope you're not squeamish."

"I'm not!" Woody bragged. The rest of the afternoon, Woody talked about what was going to happen. "Wait till you see! It's amazing to watch what happens to the chicken." Bonnie could think of nothing good about it and told him so.

"You're just a chicken yourself," he taunted. "You live on a farm, but you can't accept what happens on a farm. You're not a *real* farm girl. You're a sissy!"

"I am not a sissy!" Bonnie retorted crossly. "You're just being mean, and I don't want to talk about it any more!"

"That's fine with me!" Woody said peevishly. For the rest of the day, he ignored Bonnie and played with Paula, which irked Bonnie but made Paula quite happy.

The next morning Bonnie and Woody had no time to quarrel. Mommy put them both to work, ordering, "Get busy! We only have one day to get this house spic and span."

They vacuumed and swept the floors, dusted the furniture, and then carried an old table and chairs in from the shed, cleaned them off and set them up. They were finishing a lunch of peanut butter and jelly sandwiches when Mommy began muttering to herself, "Let's see, I still have to iron my lace tablecloths, polish the silverware, wash the crystal...." Bonnie and Woody forgot their differences and made a beeline to the kitchen door, scrambling to get outside before Mommy could put them to work again.

All afternoon they played. Woody didn't mention the chickens again until Daddy came home from work. The minute he stepped out of the car, Woody ran up to him and asked, "Are you going to catch the chickens now?"

"I have to do my regular chores first. Then I want to hone my hatchet. I don't like to see any of God's creatures suffer. A sharp blade makes sure the job is done swiftly, before the poor chicken knows what happened to him."

Woody decided to go with Daddy to do the chores. Bonnie sat down under the oak tree and stared at the wide tree stump by the chicken house. It was scarred with hatchet marks. Part of her cringed, but the other part said *Woody's right. You're a*  *farm girl, not a dumb prissy city girl who doesn't realize where her food comes from. You know this is how God intended it to be. It's time you grow up and face facts.* It took Daddy and Woody an hour to finish the chores and sharpen the hatchet. It took Bonnie equally as long to decide she would stay and see this through until the bitter end.

When Daddy and Woody saw her by the stump, they both looked surprised. "You're staying?" Daddy marveled.

"I'm staying!" Bonnie said, sounding braver than she felt.

While Daddy and Woody went to catch the first chicken, Bonnie ran to the house, told Mommy to start the water boiling, and carried the washtub from the shed to the porch.

When she arrived back at the stump, Daddy and Woody were already there. Daddy held the squawking chicken by both legs, with its neck and head lying over the stump. In his other hand was the ax. He wasted no time. He raised the ax and with one powerful blow, severed the chicken's neck in two. The squawking stopped abruptly and blood flowed down the tree stump. In spite of her determination, Bonnie had to turn away. She would have run away if Woody had not been there. Her stomach churned and she swallowed hard, putting her hand over her mouth to keep from throwing up.

"It's always hard the first time," Daddy soothed her.

Suddenly, the most amazing sight drew Bonnie's attention away! The headless chicken was frantically flailing about, flapping its wings, and running around in circles!

Woody laughed uproariously. "I told you so," he gloated.

Daddy smiled too, but then explained. "It's a reflex reaction. It takes a while until the nerves die. It gives you an eerie feeling the first time you see it happen."

Bonnie stood glued to the spot, unable to move, watching, until the last movement ceased. But in spite of the dead chicken's fascinating dance, when Daddy went to catch the next chicken, she decided she had been brave enough for one day and headed back to the house. Woody trailed after her, carrying the headless chicken by its legs.

Mommy was on the porch filling the washtub with buckets of scalding water. When the tub was full, she took the chicken from Woody and, holding it by its legs, dunked its lifeless body into the water. She held it under with a wooden spoon for a few seconds, stirring it around. A horrible stench, like burning hair, permeated the air. Bonnie and Woody held their noses in disgust. Mommy pulled the chicken out and began to pluck its feathers. It was surprising how easily they came off. By the time Daddy had the second chicken ready, the first one was plucked and ready to be cleaned out.

Bonnie and Woody followed Mommy as she carried the naked chicken into the house and put it in the sink. When Mommy grabbed a knife and began cutting around its neck, Woody piped up, "Yuck! Now this is the part *I* don't like. Taking the innards out." He hurried outside.

Bonnie laughed, calling after him, "Now who's a sissy?"

Paula charged into the kitchen. "What's all the commotion about?" But after only a minute of watching Mommy work, Paula and Bonnie stared at each other in horror and ran for the door. Woody was right. Gutting chickens was awful!

Bonnie and Woody spent the next hour taking turns riding her bike down the barn hill as Paula screamed with delight in the attached wagon. Then Mommy called them back inside.

The odor of burnt feathers hung in the air, but the sink was clean. After supper, Mommy glanced anxiously at the clock. "The chickens are ready, but we still have lots to do. There's the stuffing, the fruit salad, and the pies to make!"

"Now, Annabell, my sister and her family are simple folk. Maybe you're going a little overboard," Daddy cautioned.

"No, I'm not!" Mommy replied in the voice she used when there was no use arguing with her. "Everything must be perfect!" Daddy didn't say another word, but Bonnie sensed he was uncomfortable with all the fancy doings.

All evening they worked. Bonnie and Woody chopped onions and celery for the stuffing, and Paula tore up the bread. Mommy added the rest of the ingredients and blended them in while Daddy put Paula and the boys to bed. Woody mixed the dough for the lemon meringue pie, and Bonnie beat the egg whites. Then Mommy ordered them to bed too.

"I'll finish the pies," she said, yawning. She looked tired as she turned back to her work. But early the following morning when Bonnie came downstairs, she was peeling potatoes and both tables were already set for lunch.

"Wow, how beautiful!" Bonnie couldn't help exclaiming. There was a bouquet of fresh flowers in the center of each table with rose-colored candles on either side of them. The crystal goblets, good china, and polished silverware gleamed. There were even fancy rose-covered cloth napkins.

"Please take the little ones out to play," Mommy ordered. "I have the house clean and I want it to stay that way."

Bonnie was so busy watching the little ones and playing with Woody that she was surprised when Daddy arrived home from work. "Go in and wash up," he told everyone.

A delicious, mouth-watering aroma filled the house. Mommy was placing stemmed crystal dishes of fruit salad at each plate. She had fixed her hair and changed into a pretty rose and blue striped dress. She looked radiant and beautiful!

"We're ready," she said, smiling broadly, as she placed the last dish on the table. "Now all we need are our guests."

A half-hour passed by while Mommy fretted. "If they don't get here soon, the food will be ice cold." Finally, they heard gravel crunching in the driveway. Mommy sighed with relief. "Sit up, everyone. We'll start as soon as they come in."

Everyone was settled by the time the knock on the door came. Mommy scrambled to open it, and there stood Uncle Elwood. "Hi, everyone," he greeted them. "Is Woody ready to...?" His voice trailed off, and his mouth dropped open.

"Where are Marylou and the kids?" Mommy asked, sticking her head out the door, looking both ways in disbelief.

"They...they didn't come along," Uncle Elwood stuttered.

"But...I...I...invited you all to lunch," Mommy stammered.

Uncle Elwood shrugged helplessly. "No one told me. There must have been some mix-up. Marylou's feeling a little under the weather, so she decided to stay home with the girls. She never mentioned lunch." He squirmed uncomfortably and confessed without thinking, "I ate before I came."

Nobody said a word. Uncle Elwood realized he had made matters worse and tried again. "I'm sorry, Annabell. The table looks wonderful. You must have gone to a lot of trouble."

Mommy managed a weak smile. "It's okay. These things happen...." Her voice cracked and died away.

Uncle Elwood looked miserable. Then suddenly, his face brightened. "Hey, this looks like a feast fit for a king, and I can always eat. Woody and I would love to stay for lunch. I'll just call Marylou and explain why we'll be late."

"That's a great idea," Daddy said, trying to make the best of things. "It would be a shame to waste all this scrumptious food. There'll just be more for us to eat, that's all."

While Uncle Elwood talked to his wife, Woody whispered to Bonnie, "Your mom really looks upset."

"She is!" Bonnie replied, but didn't try to explain. What did boys understand about things like this?

Uncle Elwood finished his call and sat down. "Marylou says she thought you said, 'Come for lunch if you want to,' meaning she should call you if we were going to come. She's so sorry about the miscommunication. She had no idea you were going to all this trouble, or she'd be here, sick or not."

Mommy tried to downplay how upset she was. "It's just a meal." Her voice sounded hollow and unconvincing.

Daddy spoke up. "Well, let's say grace and eat this delicious meal before it gets cold." They bowed their heads, and Daddy began praying. "Dear Jesus, thank you for this beautiful spring day and all your many blessings. We especially want to thank you for this bountiful meal Annabell has prepared and for our guests Elwood and Woody...." Suddenly a loud wailing sound erupted, followed by deep muffled sobs. Bonnie heard a chair screech and then the bathroom door closing.

Daddy uttered an abrupt "Amen," then said, "She's just disappointed. Don't worry. She'll be fine." In a cheerier voice, he added, "Dig in. Annabell's fruit salad is delicious."

Everyone began eating, pretending things were normal. Bonnie stared at the empty places at the table and thought of the chickens that had been sacrificed and all the hours of preparation that had gone into this extravagant dinner. Uncle Elwood talked and kidded with Daddy, but Bonnie saw both of them glance toward the bathroom door several times before Mommy finally reappeared. Her face was red and her eyes were puffy, but when she spoke, she was in control of her voice. "Here, let me take those," she offered, gathering up the empty fruit salad dishes. "Bill, would you carve the chickens while I put the other dishes on the table?"

The rest of the meal went off without a hitch. Everything was delicious, but no one really enjoyed it. Even little Billy knew something was not right and didn't eat as much as usual. Uncle Elwood took big helpings of everything and ate every bite, saying over and over how wonderful it all was. "Lemon meringue pie!" he exclaimed when Mommy served the dessert. "I'll take a big slice of that." But Bonnie could tell it was all he could do to finish it.

Finally, the fiasco was over. As soon as it was sociably acceptable, Uncle Elwood and Woody departed. Daddy seemed happier than usual to go and help Mr. Ivan. The little ones scooted off into the living room to play. Only Mommy and Bonnie were left, sitting in the midst of a kitchen full of dirty dishes and wrecked dreams. Mommy stared at the wall for a while and then broke into deep heart-wrenching sobs.

Somehow, Bonnie knew enough to let her cry. Most people would probably think it was crazy to cry over such a minor thing as a spoiled dinner. Bonnie knew something they didn't. Due to her lack of education, Mommy worried she might not do things well enough. To compensate for this, she did everything to perfection. To fail so miserably, especially at one of her best talents, was unforgivable. Although it was nobody's fault, to her, it was the ultimate humiliation. And that it happened with people she wanted so desperately to impress made it almost unbearable.

Mommy stood up. She appeared exhausted, but all she said was, "Let's get this mess cleaned up." After that night, she never mentioned the spoiled dinner again. If someone brought it up, she simply said, "I don't want to talk about it."

It's funny how sometimes the simplest things can cause us so much pain.

Chapter 6

GOOD THINGS IN THE SPRING

"What a wonderful service!" Mommy exclaimed as they rode home from church on Easter Sunday. They were the most positive words she had spoken since the disappointing dinner over a week ago. It was good to see her smile.

Sunshine flooded the Oldsmobile's interior. Outside, fluffy white clouds floated by in a brilliant blue sky. Warm breezes scented with clover wafted in the open windows.

Bonnie breathed in the pleasant aroma and relaxed in the back seat beside Paula. It *had* been an inspiring service. Ever since Christmas, the youth choir, along with the adult choir, had been practicing for this morning's Easter cantata. Bonnie had never sung in such a difficult presentation before, but all their hard work paid off. The songs were beautiful and the pageantry awesome as together they told the miraculous, life-changing story of Jesus' death, burial, and resurrection.

Mommy spoke again. "It isn't that I don't appreciate Rev. Mark's sermons, but there's something about music that reaches the soul in a way words can't."

Thinking about the deep spiritual feelings the production evoked in her own spirit, Bonnie had to agree. For the first time, she understood the importance of music in worship. She understood too, that the piano lessons she hated so much might not be a total waste of time after all.

A few days after Easter, the lovely weather suddenly disappeared; the temperature dropped, the skies turned dark, and it poured rain. "It feels like winter again," Bonnie grumbled after the second day of cold, inclement weather.

Mommy agreed. "I'm tired of dark, dreary days, and nothing smells worse than pig manure on a rainy day. I can't wait to get off this smelly farm."

"Now, girls," Daddy said, looking up from his newspaper. "Remember, April showers bring May flowers, and the rain's good for the crops Ivan and I just planted."

"That may be," Mommy went on, "but I see how tired you've been lately, Bill. Your job, the machinist training, and then the farm chores on top of it all—it's too much."

"Ivan did complain again the other day," Daddy admitted. "He doesn't like it that I can't help on Saturday mornings."

"See what I mean?" Mommy said, pressing her point. "Isn't there any way we could afford the down payment on a place of our own?"

"You know there isn't," Daddy said firmly. "Besides, I'm committed to Ivan for the next year. I can't go back on my word."

Mommy sighed in disappointment. Bonnie sighed with relief.

"Here's something that will cheer you up," Daddy said, showing Mommy an article from the paper. "A man named Salk has found a vaccine that is supposed to prevent polio."

"That is good news!" Mommy said, brightening. "I guess all the money people gave to research a cure paid off."

Bonnie would never forget the picture she had seen years ago of a room full of children in iron lungs, unable to breathe without being encased in the steel contraptions, not to mention all those who died or were crippled by the terrible disease. She was glad she had filled her March of Dimes folder with dimes every time the school sent one home.

"It says Salk is going to donate the vaccine," Daddy continued. "In the near future, they plan to give injections of it in the schools, hoping to eradicate the disease."

"Injections?" Bonnie cringed. As much as she wanted to see the disease stopped, she was afraid of needles.

"It's better than getting polio," Daddy reminded her.

Remembering the picture, Bonnie decided to be brave.

Later that evening, just as the rain finally let up, the telephone rang. After Daddy hung up the phone, he made an announcement. "Great news! I'm going to be an uncle again. Marylou is expecting a baby." Immediately, it dawned on Bonnie that this was probably the reason Aunt Marylou hadn't come to Mommy's dinner. She had morning sickness.

Mommy didn't mention that fact, however, when she answered Daddy. "First, your sister Anne, then my brother Sammy's wife, Arlene, and now Marylou. That's three pregnancies already this year, and it's only April." Mommy stopped and counted on her fingers before continuing. "During the past four years, between your family and mine, about a dozen babies have been born!"

"That's what happens with large families like ours," Daddy said, laughing. "They just keep multiplying."

Bonnie had noticed her number of cousins rapidly increasing. She really didn't mind. It was rather nice to be a part of a large, extended family. However, when it came to her own family, she thought it was perfect just the way it was.

The following day, beautiful spring weather returned. By Saturday, the soil was dry enough to plant the garden. Mr. Ivan gave Daddy the afternoon off, and the whole family worked putting in seeds and vegetable plants. Gardening was a necessity, not a hobby, but in spite of the hard work, it was one of Daddy's favorite things to do. He sang, whistled, or hummed merrily as he hoed and planted. Whenever Bonnie worked near him, he sang, "My Bonnie Lies over the Ocean." He had a special tune for each of his children and one for Mommy called "Lonesome for You, Annabell." As he tended his vegetable garden, Daddy was planting another kind of seed, the seeds of love.

While the garden took root, the next week slipped swiftly by, filled with the usual activities. On Monday was Good

News Club; on Tuesday, the after-school program; on Wednesday, prayer meeting; on Thursday, choir practice; and on Friday, piano lessons. In addition, there were the daily chores: babysitting, homework, and piano practice. And just before bedtime each evening came Bonnie's favorite activity—watching television with the family.

At school, things were winding down toward the end of what had been a good year for Bonnie. She had managed to stay in the top math group, and her grades were good in all her subjects. She and her three close friends were getting along well too. Sheila now attended church with Kathy, and they had become best friends. Bonnie and Barbara, who rode the bus together and were both in Mrs. Sabo's class, had also bonded. Every day at recess and lunch the four of them got together and caught up on each other's news.

The latest topic of discussion was the upcoming class trip to Philadelphia. Barbara had been there, but the rest had not. In their excitement, they bombarded her with questions.

"I don't know," Barbara said one day, exasperated from trying to answer the same questions every day. "I told you, I was only six years old. I can hardly remember anything."

"Well, I know one thing for sure," Kathy said. "I'm going to buy a souvenir for my room."

"Me too!" Barbara said. "A model of the Liberty Bell."

"You have your own rooms?" Bonnie asked, surprised. She had never heard them mention this fact before.

"Sure! Don't you?" Barbara asked.

"No...." Bonnie replied, but before she could elaborate on the subject, the bell rang, ending recess. As she and her friends hurried back to their classrooms, Bonnie made two decisions. She was going to buy a souvenir, but more importantly, she was going to have a room of her own! She could hardly wait until school was over, so she could go home and ask Mommy about it.

Chapter 7

BONNIE WANTS HER OWN ROOM

Bonnie hopped off the school bus and raced the whole way home. Mommy was in the living room vacuuming.

Breathlessly, Bonnie blurted out, "I want my own room!"

Mommy cupped her hand behind her ear, indicating she couldn't hear. "Wait a minute. I'm almost finished."

Bonnie paced impatiently until Mommy switched off the noisy machine, and then asked again, more politely this time. "Please, may I have my own room?"

Mommy looked bewildered. "What brought this on?"

"Barbara and Kathy have their own rooms."

"Oh, I see." Mommy thought for a moment while Bonnie held her breath. "I'll consider it," she said at last, but her voice sounded doubtful.

Disappointed, Bonnie begged, "We have empty bedrooms upstairs at the back of the house. Can't I have one of them?"

"Those two rooms are full of storage boxes and neither room has any flooring, blinds, or curtains. You would need bedroom furniture. All of these cost money we don't have."

Having her own room had seemed like such a simple request. She had not even considered the cost. Still, it was so important to her, she decided to try again.

"But..." she began.

"No 'buts'," Mommy said in her I-mean-business voice. "I said I would think about it, and I will, but don't get your hopes up. Please put the vacuum away for me."

Obediently, Bonnie unplugged the vacuum, rolled up the cord, and carried it to the shed. She knew better than to say anything more, but for the rest of the evening, she pouted.

That night she was surprised when Daddy appeared at her bedside shortly after Mommy tucked her and Paula in bed. "What's this I hear about your wanting your own room?"

Immediately, Bonnie began complaining, "All my friends have their own rooms. I'm tired of being poor. It's not fair."

"I'm afraid you're going to find out life isn't always fair," Daddy rebuked her. "We don't always get what we want."

"But we have two empty rooms!" Bonnie wailed.

"Yes," Daddy replied, "Exactly right. They're empty! That's the problem. What it would cost to fill them with the things you'd need would buy food, clothing, and shoes for the family. Do you think a room is more important than that?"

"No," Bonnie muttered, but in her heart, she only cared about getting a room of her own.

"You're old enough now to understand these things, Little Bird," Daddy continued, softening his words by using his pet name for her. "It's not that we don't want you to have nice things, but it isn't always possible. Try to accept that fact. It will make your life a lot easier." He tucked the covers around her, kissed her lightly on the cheek, and was gone.

Paula, who had been quietly lying beside her in the double bed, spoke out of the darkness. "Are you mad at me?"

Startled, Bonnie asked, "No, why do you think that?"

"Because you don't want to sleep in the same bed with me anymore," Paula responded, sounding upset.

"It isn't that...." Bonnie tried to explain, but she really didn't know why having her own room was so important to her. It just was. "You'll understand when you're older."

Paula, who usually would not have settled for such a wishy-washy answer, seemed satisfied. "Someday I want to have my own room too," was all she said. Her statement surprised Bonnie. Paula was growing up and changing too.

A few minutes later, as Bonnie lay in the darkness, half-asleep and still sulking, Paula spoke again. "Did you pray about it?"

"No," Bonnie had to admit. She had not even said her usual evening prayers. She was too upset.

"I'll pray for you," Paula offered and before Bonnie could agree, she began to ask God to find a way to give her big sister her own room. She said, "Amen," yawned, and added, "But I'll be lonely in this big bed without you."

Although they slept in the same bed night after night, Bonnie had not given her younger sister a hug in a long time. She turned over and hugged her hard. "Thanks!"

"You're welcome," Paula replied and almost before the words were out of her mouth, she was asleep. Bonnie lay in the darkness thinking about Paula. Sometimes she could be so stubborn that it drove her crazy, but she had a good heart.

At home, Bonnie didn't say another word about the room. At school on Monday, however, she complained bitterly about it all day. Sheila tried to console her, reminding her that she didn't have her own room either. Her house only had two bedrooms, and they were full. Her older brother had to sleep on the living room couch. It should have made Bonnie feel better, but it didn't. After all, her house had five bedrooms, and two of them were empty.

The next day, Kathy took Bonnie aside. "Remember when I first came to this school? You and I agreed we would try to win our friends to Jesus." Bonnie nodded, wondering what she was getting at. "Sheila is a Christian now, but Barbara isn't. I don't think your attitude about your room is a very good testimony to her."

Bonnie felt her face getting hot. How dare Kathy accuse her of being a bad testimony! "I just want my own room. Is that too much to ask?" Bonnie retorted angrily.

"No," Kathy replied understandingly. "I love having my own room, and I see how important it is to you to have a place of your own, especially with two younger brothers and a sister bugging you. But you're usually so happy, and yesterday you did nothing but...but complain."

"I did?" Bonnie was shocked.

Kathy nodded. "Barbara even mentioned it to me. And think how it makes Sheila feel when you constantly talk about it. She'll never be able to have a room of her own."

It dawned on Bonnie that Kathy was trying to tell her, as nicely as she could, that she was being selfish and inconsiderate. Kathy never said anything deliberately hurtful, so it must be true. Thinking back on it, Bonnie now realized it *was* true, and her anger melted away. She cringed in shame, remembering how badly she had behaved the day before.

"Is that why you have never talked about having your own room before?" Bonnie asked, suddenly realizing Kathy was an only child and must have had her own room all her life, yet she never flaunted it in her friends' faces.

"Yes," Kathy confessed, "but I do hope you get your own room someday too." She grabbed Bonnie's hand. "For now, though, let's forget about rooms and go play with the others."

That night, for the first time since she begged Mommy for her own room, Bonnie said her prayers. She confessed her bad attitude, prayed for her friends, especially Barbara's salvation, and thanked God for the roomy farmhouse and the people in it she loved. She did ask God to please, please find a way to give her a room of her own. But she added a promise: She would wait without griping or complaining, and, as hard as it might be, she would accept a "no" if that's what her parents decided.

Chapter 8

AN UNUSUAL CELEBRATION

Bonnie was determined to keep her promise. Although she still desperately wanted her own room, she no longer moped about the house, and she stopped mentioning it at school.

The last day of April fell on Saturday, and Daddy, Bonnie, and Paula again worked in the garden, this time hoeing weeds. It was hard work, and as the afternoon wore on, Bonnie and Paula often took breaks to rest their aching arms or nurse their blisters. Finally, seeing all the rows they still had to do, Bonnie complained, "Why isn't Mommy helping?"

"Mommy had another project to work on this afternoon," Daddy said with a gleam in his eye.

Bonnie was curious. "What project?"

"You'll see," he said. "I'll finish up. You girls go sit on the lawn swing until Mommy calls you for supper."

Glad to be free, Bonnie and Paula dashed to the swing. As they sat facing each other, gently swinging back and forth, Bonnie asked Paula, "Do you know what Mommy's doing?"

"No, but I saw her and Daddy whispering together."

What could it be? They would just have to wait and see.

Mommy's face was beaming when she called them in for supper. The table was nicely set and a decorated cake sat on the counter. "Happy Seventh Anniversary!" she exclaimed.

Bonnie was stunned. Always before, they had celebrated the anniversary of their moving to the farm and Paula's birthday at the same time. But this year they had already celebrated Paula's birthday a week ago on its actual date. Bonnie had assumed Mommy was going to ignore the anniversary, since she wasn't happy on the farm anymore.

Mommy seemed to read Bonnie's mind and explained with a laugh, "As you can see, I didn't forget the anniversary. I just thought Paula was old enough to have her special day all to herself. There's another reason too. This year, there's a surprise that goes along with our anniversary celebration."

"I know the surprise," little Billy piped up.

"Shhh! Remember. It's a secret." Mommy cautioned him.

All through the celebration supper, Bonnie wondered what the surprise could possibly be. Finally, Mommy stood up and said dramatically, "I have an announcement to make…."

"Mommy moved all the boxes! That's the surprise!" little Billy interrupted, smiling smugly at knowing the answer.

"What?" Bonnie and Paula looked at each other, puzzled.

"Actually that is part of it," Daddy informed them, laughing, "but I think Billy's in for his own surprise."

"Follow me!" Mommy ordered. She snatched up baby Tommy and led the family upstairs and into Billy's room.

"Oh!" Billy squealed in delight when he saw his room. His bed had been moved closer to the far wall, and on it was a new bedspread. It was blue with green tractors, yellow trucks, and red fire engines all over it. Next to it, on the floor, lay another spread, and on the windows were matching curtains.

Mommy said, "Tommy is two-and-a-half years old. He no longer needs the crib in our room. We're getting him his own bed and from now on, this will be the boys' room."

"I like it!" Billy yelled, and hopped up on his bed.

"Me too!" Tommy cried. He squirmed from Mommy's arms, ran to the bedspread on the floor, and flopped down.

Mommy laughed, pleased at their reaction. "I decorated it today after their naps while they played downstairs."

"Now follow me," Daddy said, grinning. He led them into one of the back bedrooms. To Bonnie's amazement, the boxes were cleared out. The room was newly carpeted and on the windows hung the lace curtains that used to be in Billy's room. Unable to believe it, she asked, "Is…is this for me?"

"It sure is! I sneaked around all day yesterday, trying to move the boxes without any of you finding out, but Billy managed to see me doing it," Mommy said, laughing.

"Oh, thank you!" Bonnie cried, hugging Mommy tightly.

"Hey, what about me?" Daddy said, pretending to be upset. "I put the carpet in last night while Mommy and you kids were at the grocery store and piano lessons. Jiminy fires! Did I have to work fast! Don't I get a hug?"

Of course, Bonnie gave him a big hug too. "Thank you!"

"There's no bed!" Paula noted. "Where will she sleep?"

"We're going to the used furniture store right now to buy Tommy's bed and Bonnie's bed and bureau," Daddy said.

Bonnie was speechless with happiness, but the boys made up for it. "Yippee!" yelled Billy. "Yippee!" repeated Tommy.

There was no "Yippee" from Paula. She turned and walked out of the room. Daddy followed her, silently motioning everyone else to come along. Paula sat on the double bed in the hallway bedroom, looking sad and dejected.

"What's wrong?" Daddy asked her.

"I don't want to sleep alone," Paula cried out.

"There's a surprise for you too," Mommy consoled her.

Paula's face brightened. "There's something for me?"

"You betcha!" Daddy replied. "But first, I want to tell you something. I don't think you figured this out. But, since Bonnie is moving out, this will be *your* own room."

By the surprised look on her face, Bonnie realized Paula had not thought of that, but then, neither had she.

Paula cried out in joy, "Yippee! I have my own room too," forgetting all about being lonely.

Daddy continued, "And, since you're going to school next year, how would you like to pick out a desk for your room?"

"My own desk! Oh, boy!" Paula shrieked in joy.

"I'm glad you're happy, but there is something I need to tell you," Mommy cautioned. "In the winter, it will be freezing in that back room. Bonnie will have to move back in here. I don't want any complaints out of you two when the time comes. Is that clear?"

Bonnie nodded. She would rather be in the cozy double bed cuddling up with Paula during the freezing winter nights. Paula nodded too, and Bonnie knew she felt the same.

"Okay. Let's go!" Daddy said. "We'll borrow Ivan's truck and pick up the furniture. Tomorrow after church we'll set everything up."

It didn't take long to pick out the furniture. With a whoop of joy, Paula found her desk right away. It was white with flowered designs on its drawers. While Daddy searched for Tommy's bed and Bonnie selected her bedroom suite, Paula stood guard over her desk, making sure no one else bought it.

Mommy and Bonnie spent the next afternoon decorating her room. In her joy, Bonnie didn't mind the boys' getting in the way, or Paula's calling her and Mommy every few minutes to come and see what she was putting in her desk.

Bonnie's new room didn't have much furniture, just a bed, dresser, and an old wardrobe from the attic, but with the pretty flowered bedspread Mommy found in one of the storage boxes and a few fancy doilies, it suited her just fine.

As Mommy tucked her in that night, Bonnie asked the question that had been on her mind the past few days. "I thought you couldn't afford to give me my own room?"

Mommy smiled. "We were planning to get Tommy a bed with this year's tobacco check. When it came, it was more than we expected. By then, you had such a good attitude; we decided you deserved your own room. We didn't want to leave anyone out, so we made it a celebration for everyone."

After Mommy left, Bonnie snuggled under the covers and sighed in contentment. As she lay there, enjoying her new room, it occurred to her how much time and effort her parents had put in the past few days to give her and her siblings this wonderful surprise. She also concluded that God had answered her prayer—but not before she changed her attitude.

Chapter 9

A TRIP TO PHILADELPHIA

In mid-May, the highly anticipated trip to Philadelphia arrived at last. Daddy dropped Bonnie off at school early that morning. Two tour buses were already there, along with the teachers, chaperones, and most of the fifth grade students.

"Hurry!" Barbara hollered excitedly, grabbing Bonnie's hand and pulling her toward one of the buses. "Kathy and Sheila are saving us seats across from them."

The inside of the bus was luxurious with padded seats, upholstered in dark gray with a thick blue diagonal stripe across each one. "This sure beats our school bus," Barbara said, sinking down into the window seat. Bonnie nodded in agreement and settled comfortably into the seat beside her. During the two-hour ride, the four friends talked of nothing else but what they were going to see, do, and buy.

Their first stop was Valley Forge, where the Continental Army spent the winter of 1777, during the Revolutionary War. Viewing a replica of the tiny, unheated log cabins that had each housed twelve starving, poorly clad soldiers, it was easy to understand why they suffered from frostbite and all kinds of diseases. Many died during that "Winter of Despair."

What affected Bonnie the most, however, was a remark their tour guide, Mr. Wiser, made about the character of their leader, George Washington. "It is said General Washington was a man of prayer. People reported seeing him on his knees or reading his Bible, searching for God's wisdom."

After the sobering tour, they piled back on the bus and traveled the short distance to Philadelphia. The bus dropped them off at Betsy Ross's narrow two-story house where they watched a reenactment of Betsy's making the first American flag. It had thirteen red and white stripes and thirteen stars. All four friends purchased souvenir flags.

The whole group walked to a nearby restaurant. When she stepped inside, Bonnie felt as if she had traveled back in time to the 18th century. The atmosphere was old-fashioned, and the items on the menu had British-sounding names. But the food was inexpensive and good, and it was fun to eat from pewter dishes and drink colas out of ale mugs.

After lunch, they visited Independence Hall and the Liberty Bell. The guide explained, "The Liberty Bell was rung on July 8, 1776, to announce the adoption of the Declaration of Independence. It cracked while ringing soon after it was cast. It was recast and cracked again. After that, it was seldom rung." He read the inscription embossed on the bell. *Proclaim Liberty throughout all the land unto all the inhabitants thereof.* Bonnie, Kathy, and Sheila were impressed when he told them it was a quote from the Bible. Again, all four friends purchased souvenirs.

Their last stop was the Franklin Institute, where they spent quite a while exploring the interesting displays. Everyone's favorite was the giant walk-through replica of a human heart. It was awe-inspiring to walk inside this two-story organ.

At first, on the bus ride home, it was noisy with everyone talking at once, but soon the bus grew quiet. Bonnie's friends fell asleep, exhausted from the long day, but she could not. The day's events kept spinning around in her head.

It was after eight by the time they arrived back at the school. All the way home, Bonnie told Daddy about the marvelous trip. At home, Mommy hurried Bonnie to bed, but she was still by her bedside ten minutes later as Bonnie chattered on about the trip. After Mommy left, Bonnie felt herself drifting off. Her last thought was of Washington's prayers. She was sure they were the reason why the United States won the war.

Chapter 10

TWO CAMPS

The last weeks of school flew by, and it was time for Bonnie and her friends to part, but they had the summer to look forward to, and in the fall, they would be together again.

No sooner had school ended than it was time for church camp. Almost all of the kids from the Junior Sunday School Department were going, and excitement ran high.

Daddy dropped Bonnie off at the church on Sunday afternoon. Sara Jane, a long-time friend, ran up to her and begged, "Ride in my car." When all the children and their luggage were loaded, the caravan took off for Camp Gretna.

After registering at the camp office, the boys left for their cabins on one side of the complex. The girls climbed the hill on the other side to a large three-story house.

Sara Jane and Bonnie were assigned to a dorm on the first floor. "Hi, I'm Judy Hess," the counselor greeted them pleasantly. "Find a bunk and get settled. Supper's in an hour."

Sara Jane picked a top bunk and Bonnie took the bottom. They unpacked, changed into dresses, and got to know their roommates. By the time the dinner bell rang, they were friendly enough to hurry down the hill as a group.

At supper, they were assigned tables of four boys and four girls plus a counselor. After the meal, they sang fun songs, played silly games, and watched a skit. Then they walked to vespers—an inspiring, early evening worship service held in an outdoor tabernacle. Afterward, they went to their dorms, changed into play clothes, and hurried back for snack time.

Bonnie knew the first evening that the nightly campfires were going to be her favorite thing. The flickering firelight was mesmerizing, and along with the star-filled sky, the crickets chirping, and the tangy aroma of burning wood, it created an aura of peace and a feeling of God's presence. They sang quiet, worshipful choruses, and the camp director challenged them to live lives dedicated to God.

The next morning, they rushed to get dressed and clean the dorm before breakfast. The rooms were inspected for neatness every day, and the winners were announced at lunch.

After breakfast, each table group headed for a different area of the woods for a Bible study. Afterward, each child went off alone for a time of reflection and prayer. As the week went on, Bonnie grew to like this quiet alone time more and more. She also enjoyed the craft time that followed. She made a plaque for her room that read "GOD IS GOOD."

At lunch, Bonnie and her roommates groaned with disappointment when their dorm didn't win the neatness award, but laughed uproariously when one of the boys' cabins was voted "The Messiest" and they had to clear the tables.

Next came the part of camp Bonnie hated—one hour of rest. The minute it was over, she was out of her bunk and into her bathing suit, ready for the hike through the woods to the lake. The boys were rarin' to go too. All the way to the lake, they sang funny songs at the top of their lungs and teased the girls by throwing spiders at them, making them scream hysterically. Bonnie didn't like spiders either, but she would not give the boys the satisfaction of letting them know it.

She loved swimming in the lake, especially jumping off the large rafts anchored near the shore, shouting a loud "Yahoo!" The only day during the week she didn't go swimming was the day they hiked up the mountain to Governor Dick, a one-of-a-kind 66-foot-tall concrete tower.

To reach it, the campers took a narrow trail that climbed steadily upward over a rocky and, sometimes, steep path, but no one complained. The day was beautiful, the birds chirped and sang, and wildflowers bloomed everywhere.

Bonnie was tired by the time they reached the tower, but she didn't stop. She followed the group up the steel ladders, stopping at each landing for a moment to rest her aching legs and catch her breath before going on. Up and up she went, passing eight landings before, breathless, she reached the top.

It was worth the climb! The panoramic view was awe-inspiring! One of her roommates told her that on a clear day you could see five counties. Bonnie stood transfixed until the same roommate tapped her on the shoulder and said, "Hurry up. We're leaving." Reluctantly, she started back down.

Although her dorm never won the neatness award, in spite of trying desperately hard, everything else about camp that week was great. At the campfire on the last night, each camper threw a stick into the fire as he committed the next year to the Lord. Then the camp director shocked them by asking for a night of complete silence, so that they could concentrate on the seriousness of the vow. Before they went to sleep, they were to write a letter reminding themselves of the vow. It would be mailed to them in January.

It was hard for the campers to undress and brush their teeth without talking, but no one broke the silence. As Bonnie wrote the letter, she realized, without all the usual hustle and bustle, she felt nearer to God than she had ever felt before. She prayed with all her heart that when she received the letter in January she would still feel the same way.

Tears flowed the next morning after breakfast as the campers began leaving for home. Bonnie and her new friends hugged, promising they would see each other again next year.

It felt good to be back in her own room that evening, but in the days that followed, Bonnie found herself missing the spirituality, camaraderie, and excitement of camp life. So, when Mommy asked her in early July if she wanted to attend another camp, she shouted without hesitation, "Oh, yes!"

At Camp Lou San, Bonnie stayed in a cabin with girls who were several years older than she was. One girl, Jane, already wore nylons and high heels. Bonnie felt childish next to them, but to her joy, they accepted her as one of them.

The activities were similar to the ones at the other camp, except there was no swimming, so there was more free time.

Bonnie discovered the perfect activity to fill in the extra time. A wide stream flowed by the camp. Beside it was a dirt path. Down the path, out of sight, was a tire swing that hung from a tree limb out over the water. She spent every spare moment swinging on it, enjoying the quiet solitude, and mulling over the spiritual truths she was learning.

But there was one upsetting thing about the camp—no Bermuda shorts were allowed. Mommy, unaware of this, had packed all shorts and a pair of pedal pushers. Bonnie had to wear the same pair of pedal pushers every day that week!

As the week passed by, in spite of their age difference, Jane and Bonnie became good friends. Jane was soft-spoken, slim, and pretty. Besides that, she was helpful and kind. When Bonnie confessed how humiliating it was to have to wear the same outfit every day, Jane consoled her with a hug. "Don't worry about it. I like you no matter what you wear."

The last night of camp, Bonnie couldn't help but ask Jane, "What makes you so extra nice?"

"That's easy," Jane replied. "I have Jesus in my heart. I try to treat everyone the same way He would treat them."

Bonnie had Jesus in her heart too, but she didn't always act like it. She wanted so much to be like Jane.

As Jane hugged her good-bye the next day, she whispered, "Remember—treat everyone as Jesus would." Bonnie promised that she would. She would also remember Jane and her sweet testimony for God for the rest of her life.

Chapter 11

AFTER THE CAMPS

Bonnie woke up a few days after camp, yawned, and glanced out her bedroom window just as a crow flew by. "Oh, no," she cried aloud, jumping up. "It might eat the corn!" Forgetting all about the promise she made to herself at camp to have devotions every morning before leaving her room, she dressed in a flash and scurried downstairs.

"Where's the fire?" Mommy wanted to know.

"I saw a crow! I have to make a scarecrow," Bonnie declared, heading straight for the kitchen door.

"You might want to check the garden first," Mommy suggested.

Bonnie peered out the screen door at the garden. Two scarecrows stood in front of the corn!

"How did they get there?" she asked, dumbfounded.

"I helped Daddy make them," Paula piped up proudly.

"Oh," Bonnie felt a twinge of jealousy. That had always been her job, but remembering Jane's example, instead of sulking, she turned to Paula and said, "Thanks!"

"You're welcome," Paula replied, beaming.

"If we had waited for you to come home from camp, there wouldn't be any corn left," Mommy said, laughing as she poured Bonnie a bowl of cereal. "Don't worry, there's plenty left for you to do. After you eat, I want you to pick the corn and help me husk it."

Bonnie sighed as she grabbed a bucket and headed for the garden after breakfast. She didn't really mind the work. She loved being outdoors in the fresh air, but she missed the closeness to God and the fun times she had experienced at both camps. There wasn't much time for praying or playing on a farm. It was get up, get busy, and keep busy until the work was done. And the work seemed endless.

In an hour, Bonnie picked six dozen ears of corn. Mommy brought the boys outside to play while she, Paula, and Bonnie husked the corn under the shade of the oak tree.

"Oh, by the way," Mommy said as she scrubbed an ear of corn with a vegetable brush, cleaning off the last remnants of silk, "you missed some news while you were at camp. Your Aunt Josie's pregnant again. She's due in February."

"That makes four aunts who are expecting babies!" Bonnie exclaimed. At the rate her aunts were getting pregnant, she wondered which aunt would be next!

The following week, the garden kept everyone busy. Everyday there were more vegetables ready to be picked and put up for the winter. At first, Bonnie managed to have devotions in the morning, but then Mommy began waking her up earlier since there was so much to do. Things soon settled back to the way they were before she attended the camps—reading a few Bible verses and a quick prayer before bedtime.

Treating everyone the way Jesus would was not proving to be easy either. When Billy sneaked into her room and broke her plaque from camp, the words she spoke were not Christlike at all; and when Paula refused to obey while Bonnie was babysitting, it was all she could do to hold back the angry words in her mind. And, it had never hit her before how much she complained. Often she bit her lip to stop herself from saying something negative. Sometimes it slipped out anyway. How did Jane do it? Would she ever be able to be like her?

Bonnie was discovering just how much harder it was to live for God at home in the real world than it had been in the wonderful, spiritually guided environment of camp. At the rate she was going, it would take her a lifetime to become the kind of Christian God wanted her to be.

Chapter 12

A HEAT WAVE

In late July, a heat wave moved into the area. Mommy especially minded the hot, humid weather. The longer the scorching days lasted, the more they bothered her. One day by mid-afternoon, the thermometer on the porch read 100 degrees. Sweat poured off Mommy and Bonnie as they canned tomatoes in the miserably hot kitchen. Mommy often sat down to rest. Suddenly, in the middle of putting tomatoes into a jar, she cried, "I feel sick," and ran for the bathroom.

When she returned, she looked wilted and tired. "It's too hot to work in the kitchen right now," she decided. "I'll finish up later. Take your sister and brothers outside to play where it's cooler. I want to rest for a while." A half-hour later, when Bonnie ventured back inside, to her relief, Mommy was bustling about the kitchen cleaning up the canning mess.

The next day was just as hot, and again Mommy felt sick from the heat, although this time, she managed with Bonnie and Paula's help, to finish the canning before lying down.

That night, it was unbearably hot upstairs. No one slept well. In the morning, Daddy yawned and told Mommy, "Don't worry about the garden. It's been dry lately and the vegetables aren't growing as fast. Rest up while you can."

After Daddy left for work, Mommy seemed listless. She asked Bonnie to do the breakfast dishes while she started the laundry, but an hour later, she was still sitting on the couch. After several trips to the bathroom, she finally went upstairs to gather the sheets and soiled clothing. When she came downstairs with her arms full of dirty laundry, she didn't look well.

47

"Are you okay?" Bonnie asked, concerned.

"It's just the heat," Mommy said, dropping the wash and hurrying to the bathroom.

There was something familiar about the way Mommy was acting. Bonnie had seen her like this before...but when? Vague memories stirred in her brain but would not come to the surface.

By mid-morning, Mommy was feeling better and soon had two loads of wash ready to hang up. "Bonnie, get the clothespins and help. It's beginning to cloud up. I think we'll get rain later."

She was right. In the middle of the afternoon, dark clouds began filling the sky and ominous thunder sounded in the distance. Bonnie had just taken down the last few pieces of laundry when large drops of rain began to fall.

The rainstorm washed away the sultry weather. By the time Daddy arrived home from work late that afternoon, the temperature had dropped to a refreshing eighty-two degrees.

"Now this is more like it," Daddy rejoiced. "And the garden sure needed the rain."

The family slept soundly that night in the blissfully cool upstairs and in the morning, everyone looked refreshed with the exception of Mommy. Her face was still peaked and pale. The heat wave was over, but Mommy was still sick.

If it was not the heat, what was wrong with Mommy? Worried, Bonnie was determined to figure it out. As she picked string beans in the garden that morning, she reviewed all Mommy's symptoms. Suddenly, she knew! It had been staring her in the face all along, but she had not figured it out because she had been looking in the wrong place. She had been expecting it to happen to another aunt, not to Mommy!

Mommy had morning sickness—the same sickness Bonnie now remembered her experiencing with Paula, Billy, and Tommy. Mommy was pregnant again!

Chapter 13

THE ANNOUNCEMENT

Numbly, Bonnie continued picking string beans while her brain absorbed the startling discovery. She needed to think over this unexpected turn of events, but she would wait until she could retreat to her hideout by the curve in the lane. She forced herself to concentrate on the job at hand, carefully working her way down the last row of beans. She had almost finished when Mommy came out to check on her progress.

"My bucket's full," Bonnie boasted, showing her the overflowing pail. Mommy bent down and inspected a few plants to see if all the beans that were ready were picked.

"Great job!" Mommy praised her. "You're such a good help to me lately." Bonnie smiled with pleasure.

A half-hour later, when Mommy, Bonnie, and Paula had snapped off the ends of the last beans in the bucket, Mommy rose from the kitchen table. "You girls have done enough. Run along and play. I'll call you when lunch is ready."

"Want to swing?" Paula asked as they hurried outdoors.

"No, I'm going to my hideout," Bonnie replied. Paula started to follow her. Bonnie yelled, "No. I want to be alone!"

Instantly, Paula's face clouded over, and in a flash of guilt, Bonnie realized she had not handled the situation as Jane had taught her. Trying to repair the damage, she quickly added in a much nicer voice, "I'll play with you this afternoon." She was rewarded with a big grin from Paula.

At the hideout, Bonnie settled down into the hollow between the bushes. Shut away from the world in her own little cocoon, she contemplated the uninvited changes threatening to destroy the life she knew and loved.

First, there was Mommy's decision to leave the farm, then the possibility Ivan might fire Daddy, and now another child could be coming into the family.

Bonnie liked things the way they were. She wanted to live on the farm her whole life. She wanted Daddy to stay a farmer forever. She wanted the family to continue as they were. She wanted....

Even as she said these things to herself, she realized how selfish they sounded, but it was how she felt. How could she change that? A small voice somewhere deep inside of her whispered, *By thinking of others instead of yourself.*

But Bonnie was too full of self-pity to do that. It wasn't fair. Why did things always have to change? Why couldn't Mommy be happy on the farm? Why couldn't Ivan see how hard Daddy worked for him, in spite of all the hours he put in at his regular job? Now, another child! Always before, she had been thrilled when she found out Mommy was having a baby. This time, she was caught off guard. Several times during the past year, she overheard Mommy and Daddy firmly state to each other that they felt their family was complete. What had happened to change their minds?

Then too, by the time the baby was born, she'd almost be in junior high—old enough to know how much work was involved in taking care of a baby, and old enough to be expected to help. She already helped a lot with three younger siblings. With four, would she have any time to herself?

She heard Mommy calling in the distance, telling her it was time for lunch. With her thoughts still in turmoil, she hurried back to the house. On the way, she decided not to tell Mommy she knew about the pregnancy. After all, she might turn out to be wrong.

The next few days, Mommy seemed better and Bonnie began to think she had guessed wrong, but she soon found out she had been right all along. The first day of August brought another heat wave. Poor Mommy! Bonnie had never seen her so sick and miserable, but they lived on a farm and the work must go on. Bonnie tried to help, but there was so much to do and some things were beyond her ability. Other times, she reverted to childishness and slunk away to play in the cool shade, hoping Mommy wouldn't call her in to baby-sit or do more chores.

That Friday night, the whole family went along to Manheim to purchase the weekly groceries. As they drove through Manheim, Daddy stopped in front of a building very familiar to Bonnie—Dr. Weaver's office.

"Why are we stopping here?" Paula questioned.

"Mommy has an appointment," Daddy explained. "The boys, Bonnie, and I will go to her piano lessons and then to the grocery store. Paula, you stay with Mommy. You're old enough to wait for her in the waiting room. I'll be back to pick you both up after we're done."

"But…" Paula started to say. Daddy interrupted her.

"Do as you're told. There's no time for questions now."

Obediently, Paula followed Mommy up the steps to the doctor's office, while Bonnie, Daddy, and the boys drove off.

By the time Bonnie finished her piano lesson—which didn't go well—and they had purchased the groceries—which didn't go too well either, with two little boys running around wanting to be lifted in and out of the cart or begging to buy candy—they were running late to pick up Mommy and Paula.

But when they stopped outside Dr. Weaver's office, Mommy and Paula were nowhere in sight. Daddy sent Bonnie inside to investigate. The office was packed with people, but no Mommy or Paula. She glanced down the hall and saw them at the reception desk. Mommy spied her at the same time. "I'll be there in a minute," she mouthed.

Paula ran to Bonnie and they both headed for the car. Mommy came out a minute later. As she stepped into the car, she glanced at Daddy and nodded. On the trip home, the boys chattered noisily. Paula was unusually quiet.

At home, Mommy didn't say a word about her doctor's visit; instead, she ordered everyone to bed. "It's been a long, tiring, hot day. Time to call it quits."

Soon the house was quiet. Bonnie had almost drifted off to sleep, in spite of the oppressive heat, when she was startled awake by Paula's small figure standing by her bed. "I know why Mommy went to the doctor's tonight," she whispered.

"No, you don't!" Bonnie whispered back.

"I do too!" Paula replied determinedly.

Bonnie sat up. "How do you know?"

"Dr. Weaver gave her pink and blue vitamins!" Paula retorted in a loud whisper. "Remember when Mommy was expecting Tommy; we made her take the blue ones because we wanted a boy?" Bonnie remembered, but she was surprised Paula did. She had only been four years old.

"Are you happy about it?" Bonnie wanted to know.

"I…I guess I am," Paula replied, sounding unsure. "I do know one thing. I want Mommy to take the pink pills. If there has to be another baby, I want it to be a sister this time."

Bonnie had not considered whether the baby would be a boy or a girl. After two little rambunctious boys, a sweet adorable baby girl to cuddle and love suddenly didn't sound so bad. It might even be an answer to her prayers. Maybe a beautiful baby girl would take Mommy's mind off leaving the farm.

"I want a sister too," Bonnie declared. "We have to make sure Mommy takes only the pink vitamins."

The following evening at supper, Mommy announced she was going to have another baby.

"Yea!" Billy shouted and Tommy echoed it.

Daddy beamed. "Another brother or sister for all of you."

Paula and Bonnie looked at each other and exchanged secret smiles. They knew it was going to be a baby sister.

Chapter 14

THE SEESAW

It rained on Sunday and Monday, remained cloudy a few days, and poured again on Friday and Saturday. On Sunday, the sun finally showed its smiling face, ushering in clear blue skies and gorgeous late summer days. The timing was perfect. Daddy had a week's vacation and Mommy's morning sickness had lessened. Daddy would work for Ivan every morning, and every afternoon they would do something fun.

When Bonnie, Paula, and her brothers heard the plan, they were ecstatic, all talking at once, suggesting things to do. At Bonnie's request, they spent the first afternoon having a great time swimming in the creek by her grandparents' house. The next day, to keep Billy happy, they visited the Sprecher cousins—all boys—and went to the New Holland Park to play and swim in the pool. On Wednesday, Tommy's day to pick, they headed for Kauffman's Park. All the relatives from Manheim were there. Bonnie had not seen her cousins lately and was surprised at how they had changed. Joyce and Shirley were teenagers now and more interested in boys than in playing. But after the picnic supper, they couldn't resist joining the cousins in a watermelon-seed-spitting contest. They had such fun that, afterward, Joyce and Shirley decided to forego the boys and headed for the seesaws with Bonnie.

That's when the trouble began. The enormous seesaws were made of thick wood, painted dark green, some of which had worn away, exposing bare wood. They stood very, very high off the ground, too high for the girls to climb onto them.

Joyce had a solution. "I'll pull one end down and sit on it, while you crawl up to the top of the other end."

Bonnie shook her head. She wasn't going way up there! Joyce and Shirley egged her on. "Come on. We've done it!"

Against her better judgment, Bonnie sat horsy-style in front of Joyce, facing her, and eased herself backward, up the seesaw. As she inched her way to the top, her end sank while Joyce's end rose. Bonnie clung to the board. At last, the seesaw steadied, and she breathed a huge sigh of relief.

Then they discovered a new problem—she was not heavy enough to bring herself to the ground. She could not get off!

Again, Joyce had an idea. "Just slide back down the seesaw to my side. It's actually great fun!"

"No. I'd...I'd better call my parents," Bonnie decided.

"I'll catch you at this end," Joyce promised. "Come on!"

Bonnie gazed longingly at the pavilion where her parents were sitting. She wanted to call Daddy to help her, but she would never live it down if she did. She glanced at the ground far below, and then determinedly pushed off with both hands. As she went flying down the board, a sharp, searing pain radiated through her bottom before she smashed into Joyce, knocking her backward off the seesaw, landing on top of her.

"What are you trying to do? Kill me?" Joyce cried out, pushing Bonnie off her.

"Ow!" Bonnie screamed. As she landed on her backside, something stabbed her again. Automatically, she rolled over on her side, and the pain disappeared.

Joyce's outburst turned to concern. "Are you okay?"

"I think so," Bonnie croaked. Gingerly, she reached behind her, feeling her pedal pushers for what had caused the pain. Protruding from her backside was a sliver of wood!

Embarrassed and not wanting Shirley and Joyce to know, Bonnie slowly stood up. The movement caused some pain, but she tried not to show it. "I'm fine," she insisted.

Mommy called from the pavilion. "Time to go, Bonnie. Come help me pack up the food." Joyce and Shirley's moms were calling them too, and they hurried off.

As soon as they were out of sight, Bonnie tried to pull out the splinter. All she managed to do was break off the end of it, causing considerable pain. Feeling the area, she could tell only a small sliver remained outside her pedal pushers. She hoped no one would notice.

The splinter didn't hurt much as long as she walked slowly. She decided not to tell her parents about it. Daddy used a sewing needle to dig out splinters, and it hurt! She would wait until she got home and pull it out herself. Besides, it was in a very embarrassing place!

But Bonnie had not considered the ride home in the car. The second she sat down in the back seat, the horrible pain returned. She jumped up and stood hunched over.

"Why are you standing? Sit down!" Mommy ordered. Bonnie sat down on the edge of the seat to avoid the splinter.

When they arrived home, Bonnie tried her best to hide her dilemma as she walked gingerly to the house, but she noticed Mommy watching. Once inside, she headed for the bathroom, where she tried to remove the splinter, but it would not budge.

"What's taking you so long?" Paula hollered through the door. "I need to use the bathroom."

"Go away!" Bonnie yelled back.

Suddenly, she heard Mommy's voice just outside. "What are you doing in there? Let your sister in!"

"Just a minute," Bonnie replied, straightening her clothes.

"Are you all right? You've been acting funny ever since we left the park," Mommy said as Bonnie opened the door. She held her hand to Bonnie's forehead. "No fever."

"I'm okay," Bonnie said, feeling a little guilty. She wasn't exactly lying. A splinter in the rear wasn't that serious.

"You look a little peaked, but you're probably just tired. It's been a busy day. Head up to bed."

In her bedroom, Bonnie again tried to remove the splinter with no luck. Waiting until everyone else was asleep, she tiptoed down to the bathroom to use the tweezers. But the splinter was behind her. She couldn't see well enough to grab hold of it. While she was trying to figure out what to do next, Mommy opened the door.

In one glance, she surmised the situation. "I knew something was wrong. Why didn't you tell me?" Without waiting for an answer, she took the tweezers, pinched the end of the splinter, and pulled on it. Bonnie yelped in pain.

"I got part of it, but it broke off inside. We're going to have to go to Dr. Weaver's tomorrow to get it out."

"No!" Bonnie cried. "Dr. Weaver always gives shots!"

"It must come out or it'll become infected," Mommy said firmly. "Now go to bed and try to sleep if you can."

Bonnie tossed and turned all night, more from worry about what was going to happen in the morning than from the pain of the splinter.

In the morning, Mommy drove Bonnie to Dr. Weaver's office. During the next half-hour, everything she had dreaded the night before took place. It was humiliating, it hurt, and she had to have an injection. Even the hard candy from Dr. Weaver's candy jar didn't ease the shame she felt for crying.

On the way home, nursing her sore bottom, Mommy told her something that made her feel better. "You aren't the first person this has happened to. When your Aunt Esther was a girl, the exact same thing happened to her on the very same seesaw. She also had to go to the doctor to get it taken out and from what I've heard, she cried too."

Bonnie was glad to hear she was not the only person to do such a stupid thing, nor the only one to cry like a baby at the doctor's office. One thing she did know. She would not do anything so foolish again. The next time she would stand up for herself and listen to her own common sense.

Chapter 15

THE RAFTERS

Bonnie was soon to find out, however, that standing up for yourself is much easier said than done.

While Mommy and Bonnie were at the doctor's, Daddy stayed home with the other children. To make sure Mr. Snyder didn't get upset because he had been unable to work that morning, Daddy decided he'd better work in the afternoon. The planned outing for the day was canceled.

Paula was quite upset. It had been her day to pick the activity, and she had chosen to hike to Governor Dick. Ever since Bonnie came home from camp raving about it, Paula had wanted to go. Now her hopes were dashed.

"Can we go tomorrow instead?" Paula pleaded.

"We've invited my sister Pauline and her boys over for a hot dog/corn roast tomorrow afternoon, remember?" Mommy reminded her. "We'll go to the tower another time."

Paula was not happy. "We won't go later. We're always too busy," she whined, "and besides, her boys are all older than me. They play with Bonnie, but tell me to get lost."

Paula was right about both things. The family would probably never visit Governor Dick. They mostly went to church activities, visited extended family, or stayed home. It was a rare treat for them to go on an outing. And the boys did tease Paula. They called her a baby or ignored her.

"I'll make sure they let you play this time," Bonnie promised, feeling guilty. After all, it was her fault Paula had to give up her special day. Her offer didn't cheer Paula up much, but when a sudden thunderstorm hit in the middle of the afternoon, bringing an hour of pouring rain, Paula had to admit she was glad they weren't hiking up the trail to Governor Dick, sopping wet and cold.

The next afternoon, as they waited for Aunt Pauline and the boys to arrive, in spite of the fact that the outing would have been rained out, Paula reminded Bonnie of her promise. "Don't forget, I get to play with you and the boys."

Cousin Bob, who was seventeen, decided not to come. "He had important teenage things to do," Aunt Pauline said, rolling her eyes. But Jay, fourteen, and Larry, twelve, were with her. They were not happy to hear Paula would be tagging along with them all day, but at Bonnie's insistence, they grudgingly gave in. Larry warned Paula though, "If you want to play with us, you'd better keep up."

"I'll keep up!" Paula promised.

Jay and Larry didn't visit often, but when they did, they spent their time climbing trees and playing in the barn. Even though the boys were older than they were, Bonnie and Paula had no trouble keeping up with them in the trees. They practically lived in the oak trees and knew every branch. Bonnie was secretly proud of her sister when she saw how impressed the boys were with Paula's tree-climbing ability.

Tired of that, the group headed for the top of the barn. The hay had not been harvested yet, and the pile of hay bales was low—not much good for making tunnels. Looking around for something to do, Jay eyed the rafters and suggested, "Let's go up there and walk across the barn!"

Bonnie surveyed the rows of rafters above her. They were barely wide enough to walk on and were spaced far enough apart, if she lost her balance, she might not be able to grab one. Even from the lowest rafter, it was a long way to fall!

"I'm not going up there!" Bonnie declared.

"Oh, come on!" Jay taunted. "I've helped hang tobacco in the rafters a few times. It's not as hard to balance as it looks."

Bonnie was not convinced. "My parents told us never to climb up there," she said, trying a different approach.

"That's because you were too young then. You're going on eleven years old now," Jay persisted. "Time to grow up."

Bonnie firmly shook her head. Paula pleaded, "Come on. I want to do it!"

"*You* are not doing anything!" Bonnie let her know.

"You're not my boss," Paula snapped back.

"I'm responsible for you, and you're not going up there!"

Jay and Larry were already climbing the built-in ladder up to the top of the barn. Larry called down, "Even your little sister's willing to try it. Don't be a sissy."

If there was one thing Bonnie hated being called, it was a sissy. Forgetting about listening to her common sense, forgetting about the danger, forgetting about Paula, she started up the ladder, trying not to look down. She would show those boys who was a sissy!

By the time she reached the lowest rafter, the boys had already started across. Taking a deep breath, she timidly stepped out onto the narrow beam. She had only taken a few shaky steps when, out of the corner of her eye, she saw Paula starting up the ladder.

"Get down, Paula! Don't come up!" Bonnie screamed.

"You said I could do whatever you did. And I want to walk across," Paula shouted back and kept on climbing.

The boys were already halfway across. Bonnie was frantic. If she didn't follow them right now, she'd have to go across by herself, but Paula would not stop climbing. If she fell, Bonnie's parents would never forgive her.

Bonnie tried again. "You're too young. Go back down!"

"I'm not a baby," Paula yelled back.

"Go back down!" Bonnie ordered again.

"No!" Paula hollered back stubbornly.

Paula would not stop. Bonnie had to go back. Praying she would not slip, she back-stepped to the ladder. Even though it was only a few steps, she was trembling by the time she reached it. She climbed back down, blocking Paula's way.

Although she wasn't happy about it, Paula had nowhere to go but down. When they reached the ground, Paula was so busy grumbling that she wasn't paying attention to anything else, but Bonnie glanced up just in time to catch her breath in horror. Jay had made it across, but Larry was teetering near the edge, about to fall! Just as his one leg slipped off the rafter, Jay reached out, grabbed Larry's hand, and pulled him to safety, almost losing his own footing.

Bonnie let out the breath she had unconsciously been holding. That was a narrow escape!

When they reached the ground, not realizing she had seen the near-accident, Larry bragged, "Nothing to it!" But he appeared shaken, and in the next breath, he said, "Let's get out of here!" Jay also seemed in a mighty big hurry to leave.

It wasn't until much later that night—after the corn and doggie roast was over and the boys had gone home—that it actually dawned on Bonnie how close she had come to putting herself and Paula in grave danger. If they had crossed that narrow beam, two stories up, they could easily have fallen and been seriously injured or even killed.

The first time she hadn't listened to her common sense, all she had experienced was a painful, embarrassing splinter. The second time, the consequences could have been disastrous! Suddenly, she realized what God had done. He had used Paula's stubbornness to protect them both from her foolish disobedience. Filled with gratitude, Bonnie whispered a prayer of thanks—thanks for, of all things, her stubborn little sister!

Chapter 16

THE SUNDAY SCHOOL PICNIC

In the middle of August, the church held its annual Sunday school picnic at Long's Park just outside of Lancaster. It was the big event of the year. No church member even considered not going, including Bonnie and her family. So on Saturday, in spite of the busy vacation week they had just had, the family prepared for yet another picnic.

Mommy made ham sandwiches, macaroni salad, baked beans, red eggs, chocolate cake, and cut up a watermelon.

"Plenty of good food," Mommy said as they carried it to the car. "Not like the first time we went to the church picnic."

"What do you mean?" Bonnie queried.

"You were too young to remember. We had just started to attend the church and didn't realize the food at the picnic was not provided. Every family brought its own. We showed up empty-handed. Was that embarrassing!"

"Well, by golly, we have a trunk full of goodies now," Daddy said, grinning as he packed the food into the car trunk.

As they drove out the lane, Bonnie's curiosity got the best of her and she asked, "What happened? Did you go hungry?"

Mommy laughed. "I thought we would! After Rev. Mark said grace, everyone began eating. Then they noticed we were *not* eating, but they didn't quite know what to do about it. Finally, the family at the next table took pity on us and offered us some sandwiches. All at once, everyone was giving us food. As it turned out, we had the best meal of all!"

Smiling at the way the story turned out, Bonnie relaxed in the back seat and watched the cornfields and wheat fields pass by. Soon they arrived at the tiny town of East Petersburg.

"Don't blink or you'll miss it," Daddy joked. Besides the houses, Bonnie caught glimpses of a grocery store and a bank as the town flashed by. Then they were in the country again.

Bored with the landscape, Bonnie stared at the back of Mommy's head. Her soft brown hair hung down straight and silky until it reached her neck, and then curled up in ringlets all around the bottom. Bonnie surprised herself by blurting out, "Mommy, your hair looks like a freshly mown lawn surrounded by beautiful flowers."

Mommy turned around, a pleased look on her face. "Thank you. What a poetic way to describe my hair! Maybe you'll be a writer someday."

"Oh, no! I'm going to be a missionary!" Bonnie retorted.

"You might be surprised at what God has in store for you," Mommy said as they arrived at Long's Park.

Bonnie was always impressed with how large the park was. As they drove through, they passed a wide lake dotted with ducks, green pavilions lined with picnic tables, and several play areas filled with swings, slides, and seesaws.

Daddy parked by the pavilion the church used every year. Looking around, Bonnie recognized some girls from her Sunday school class, including Sara Jane. She started to run toward them. Daddy called her back. "Your mother needs our help carrying the food and setting up our picnic table."

When they reached the pavilion, other families were already busy putting their tables in order. After exchanging pleasantries with them, Mommy and Daddy selected a table. The entire family helped set up for the picnic, and then they were free to go their separate ways until supper.

Daddy hurried off to play baseball. Mommy gathered up Paula and the boys and headed for the play area. Bonnie found her friends playing volleyball with the teenagers.

They had already picked sides, but Sara Jane saw her and waved her in. "She's on our side!" Bonnie rather reluctantly took her place beside Sara Jane. She had never played before.

Almost immediately, the volleyball flew straight toward her. Startled, she ducked. Her teammates groaned with disappointment. Embarrassed, Bonnie was determined to hit the next ball. But, to her chagrin, she missed again. Now the boys around her didn't trust her and began hitting every ball that came her way. Her side lost 15-21, and they changed sides.

The team rotated players and it was Bonnie's turn to serve. She had watched the others serving. Now she copied their style. With all her strength, she brought her arm up and hit the underside of the ball with the side of her fist. To her delight, it cleared the net and dropped between two players. She had made a point and her team cheered. The next serve, however, hit the net, and the ball was forfeited to the other side. When she rotated to the front, Sara Jane whispered, "That first serve was great! You have power!"

Encouraged, Bonnie tried harder. By the time the next game was over, she had hit the ball over the net several times and made two points while serving. Her team won 21-19. During the third game, the boys let her play any ball that came near her, and she served four balls in a row. Her team won 21-14. They had taken the series and were ecstatic.

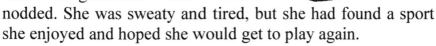

"You played a good game," Sara Jane congratulated her. Bonnie nodded. She was sweaty and tired, but she had found a sport she enjoyed and hoped she would get to play again.

Mr. Graver, the Sunday school superintendent, was calling everyone to the picnic supper. People streamed in. Soon the pavilion was full. After the strenuous game, Bonnie was hungry. Every bit of Mommy's food tasted delicious.

After everyone had eaten, Mr. Graver announced where each class would meet for their activity time, and Bonnie hurried off to her group. For an hour, they competed against their classmates in all kinds of ridiculous relay races. During the three-legged race, Sara Jane and Bonnie laughed so much that they kept falling down. Their team lost, but it didn't matter because they were having such fun.

"Time for ice cream," someone called. The entire junior Sunday school department took off running toward the pavilion. The vanilla and chocolate ice cream, packaged in little round cardboard containers and eaten with a wooden spoon, tasted deliciously cool and sweet, but Bonnie and her friends were more interested in the dry ice it was packed in.

They grabbed pellets of dry ice from the tub. The ice, when touched, burned like fire. They had a contest to see who could hold onto the hot ice the longest without dropping it. They put it in paper cups, poured water over it, and watched a cloud of steam rise up from it. But when someone suggested making a bottle bomb, a nearby adult stepped in and put a quick end to their fun, reminding them of the danger.

The sun was sinking in the sky by the time Rev. Mark called everyone back to the pavilion one last time for vespers. As daylight slowly faded away, Bonnie relaxed at the picnic table with her family, singing hymns and listening to the short devotional. Tired, but completely happy and content, Bonnie wondered if all children were as fortunate as she was to have a loving family as well as a wonderful, caring church family.

Chapter 17

BONNIE HAS QUESTIONS

"Don't take a blue one!" Paula cried out in horror one morning in late August. Mommy was about to pop a blue vitamin in her mouth.

"That's all I have left until I see Dr. Weaver tomorrow."

"Pleeease don't take it! Can't you wait until the doctor gives you more pink ones? If you take a blue pill, we might have a boy. I want another sister!"

Even though Bonnie was old enough to know vitamins had nothing to do with what sex the baby would be, somehow, it still felt safer if Mommy took the pink pills so she too pleaded, "Can't you just skip today?"

"Okay. I guess I can miss one day, but remember," she cautioned gently, "there's no guarantee it will be a girl."

"It will be!" Paula called back as she hurried outside to play with the boys on the swing.

Bonnie still had a hard time believing Mommy was pregnant. She was as slim as ever, and her morning sickness had all but disappeared. Talking about the vitamins brought to mind the question she had wanted to ask ever since Mommy announced she was going to have another baby.

Bonnie took a deep breath and blurted out, "Why are you having another baby? You said our family was complete."

"You're having a hard time accepting this, aren't you?" Mommy answered her question with one of her own.

"Yes! I think we are fine just the way we are!" Bonnie replied. "Two girls to help you and two boys to help Daddy."

"Actually, your daddy and I felt the same way, but it seems God had other plans."

Bonnie had not considered God's part in this. Shocked, she stuttered, "You mean…you mean this baby is part of *His* plan?"

"We're all part of His plan, Bonnie, Honey. Even though *we* did not plan to have this baby, God did, and He has a special purpose for this new life inside of me."

As Bonnie thought about what Mommy just said, another thing that had been bothering her came to mind. "I've heard you say that because you were both middle children in large families, you and Daddy didn't receive much attention from your parents. I don't want that to happen in our family."

"So that's what's been bothering you." Mommy put her arm around Bonnie. "First of all, let me assure you that your father and I, with God's help, are going to make sure all our children feel equally loved and cared for." She gave Bonnie's shoulder a quick squeeze before continuing. "Yes, that did happen to some extent in both our families. Grandpa Bedi had to do the best he could for his kids without a wife to help him. As for your Grandma and Grandpa Snader, well, there was a depression going on. It took most of their time and energy just to put food on the table."

"That's so sad," Bonnie cried with pity in her voice.

Mommy was having none of it. "All in all, we didn't have it that bad. Look how close we are to both our families now, plus God has given us a wonderful family of our own. We are blessed, and this baby is just another blessing."

"But…"

Mommy chuckled, knowing what Bonnie was going to say. "And, no, I don't intend to have a dozen children like my mother did. There are women who can handle that. God knows I am not one of them."

Bonnie sighed with relief. The only thing that bothered her now was the fact that the number of children in the family would be uneven. And she did so like things to be even.

Chapter 18

A NEW SCHOOL YEAR BEGINS

Mommy tore the month of August off the big calendar in the kitchen with a flourish. "School starts in a week!"

"Whoopee!" Paula yelled. She had wanted to go to school ever since she was a wee little girl and Bonnie went out the door to start first grade. Now, finally, her time had come, and she couldn't contain her joy. Mommy rummaged through Paula's dresser and wardrobe, making sure she had enough decent clothes for starting school, resulting in a shopping spree and several new pretty dresses, which only increased Paula's joy and excitement.

September 1955						
SUN	MON	TUES	WED	THUR	FRI	SAT
				1	2	3
4	5 Labor Day	6 School Starts	7	8	9	10
11	12	13	14	15	16	17
18	19	20	21	22	23	24
25	26	27	28	29	30	

Bonnie had to admit she was excited too. As much as she liked the summer, it would be great to see her friends again. And each new school year brought a fresh incentive to do her very best in her studies and make the top reading group.

Billy and Tommy were oblivious to all the school preparations. All they cared about these days was helping Daddy. Now that they were older, Daddy allowed them to tag along with him whenever he had chores to do. Everywhere Daddy went, they went. If Daddy wore a cap, they wore caps. If Daddy hitched up his pants, they hitched up their pants. If Daddy pitched hay or shoveled manure, they pitched hay or shoveled manure, although they could barely handle a pitchfork or a shovel. They walked like him, talked like him, and even drank their iced tea like him—in one long gulp, saying, "Ah, that hit the spot" afterward. No one watching could help but chuckle at the cute little imitators.

Although the first week in September was still quite hot, there was a feeling of change in the air, or maybe it was just the anticipation of fall and all the changes that come with it. As usual, Bonnie moved up to a new class in Sunday school, Good News Club started again, people began wearing darker clothing, and farmers geared up to harvest their crops.

At last, the long-awaited first day of school arrived. Bonnie rose early, but Paula was already up. Dressed in her brand-new white blouse, light blue jumper, new white socks, and shiny black patent leather shoes, Paula was pacing the kitchen, so happy and excited she could not eat breakfast.

"Bonnie, I'm counting on you to take care of your little sister today," Mommy instructed her as she and Paula went out the door. "Make sure she gets to the right class and doesn't miss the bus after school."

"I will," Bonnie promised, hurrying after Paula.

Paula darted across the yard to the lane. "We have plenty of time," Bonnie called after her, trying to get her to slow down, but Paula wouldn't lessen her pace. Breathless, Bonnie finally caught up with her at the bus stop.

Paula again paced impatiently until she saw a flash of yellow in the distance, then she shrieked, "The bus is coming! The bus is coming!" When it pulled up, she hopped on first and hurried to a seat. Bonnie followed her and sat behind her.

"Aren't you going to sit with me?" Paula sounded hurt.

"I'm sitting with Barbara. I haven't seen her all summer."

Paula looked upset until Annette climbed onto the bus at the next stop. "Paula!" Annette cried, "I forgot you started school this year" and sat down beside her.

Although Annette had always been her friend, Bonnie was glad she was sitting with Paula. Annette was actually closer to

Paula's age anyway, and as Bonnie grew older, she found she had less and less in common with Annette. Later, when Barbara got on, Bonnie was even happier because she could talk to Barbara without worrying about Paula.

Bonnie and Barbara were busy catching up on all the summer's news when the bus made an unexpected stop. A slim, attractive girl, who appeared to be their age, climbed onto the full bus and searched for an empty seat. For a moment, she glanced at them before hurrying to the back and sitting with two first grade boys.

Barbara whispered to Bonnie, "She might be in our grade. We should have asked her to sit with us."

"Maybe on the way home," Bonnie suggested. Barbara nodded in agreement.

At school, Barbara went off to their new classroom. Bonnie grabbed Paula's hand and headed for the principal's office to find out which first grade class Paula would be in.

Bonnie dreaded what Mrs. Snavely might say. She had not told Paula about mean Mrs. Winters, hoping against hope Paula would not get her for a teacher. But, now that the day had come, a premonition of doom settled over her.

Mrs. Snavely greeted them with a smile. "Hi, Bonnie. I see you brought your little sister." She studied her list. "Paula Louise Bedi, right?" Paula was speechless. Bonnie knew she was overwhelmed with her new surroundings, just as Bonnie had been on her first day of school.

"Paula, you'll be in Mrs. Winter's class. It's right next to my office." She took Paula's hand. "Let me take you there."

Bonnie's heart sank to her feet. She stood there, helpless, watching her little sister being led away to the lion's den. There was not a thing she could do about it except whisper a prayer as she rushed back to her own class.

Mrs. Ehman greeted her at the door. "Welcome to the sixth grade," she said pleasantly. She was in her early forties, tall, with short brown hair, and a no-nonsense look about her.

But Bonnie knew from her reputation that, although she was strict, she was also kind and fair.

Barbara beckoned to her. She had already picked out desks for them in the middle of the room. "Guess what? The new girl's name is Yvonne Lefever, and she's in the other sixth grade class. You'll meet her at recess."

As usual, it took over an hour just to set up the reading and math groups, hand out textbooks and workbooks, and go over the classroom rules. By then, it was time for recess.

Bonnie and Barbara joined Sheila and Kathy, who brought the new girl, Yvonne, along with them. The five of them sat on the front steps talking. Now that they were in the sixth grade and the top dogs of the school, it was beneath their dignity to play games or climb on the jungle gym.

After introducing Bonnie to Yvonne, Sheila asked, "Did Mrs. Ehman tell you about the privileges we have as sixth graders?" Without waiting for an answer, she went on. "We can use the library anytime we want, leave the grounds after school, and be in the hallway without a teacher's pass."

"And," Kathy added, "best of all, the students under us look up to and envy us!"

Yvonne spoke up. "Let's enjoy it while we can. My older brother says, when we get in high school next year, it'll all change. We'll be the ones on the bottom."

"I'm going to take advantage of every privilege! One whole year to reign and rule—yea!" Sheila gloated.

They all laughed at Sheila's enthusiasm. Bonnie surveyed her friends. They were good friends, and now it looked like Yvonne would be one of them too. She liked her new teacher, she was in the top math group again, and she was a sixth grader, admired and respected by the lower grades. Besides that, Mommy had not talked about moving for a long time now, and the new baby would be arriving sometime in late February or early March. It was going to be a good year. What could possibly go wrong?

Chapter 19

PAULA HAS A BAD TIME

After recess, Mrs. Ehman gave the class a review test to make sure they were where they needed to be in their studies. It was twelve-thirty before she finally gathered up the tests and dismissed the class for lunch. By then, Bonnie was bleary-eyed, and her stomach growled with hunger.

The younger children had already eaten, but the cafeteria line was still long. Bonnie had finally reached the front of the line and was eyeing the spaghetti and meatballs, one of her family's favorite dishes, when she heard someone calling her.

"Bonnie, please come with me," Mrs. Snavely's voice sounded urgent. "We're having trouble with your sister."

As Bonnie followed her down the hall, she saw something that confirmed her worst fears. Mrs. Winters had a vise-like grip on Paula's arm, trying to pull her forward. With the other hand, she was shaking her finger in Paula's face. Paula had both feet dug in and wasn't budging. What had Mrs. Winters done to change her sister from the happy little girl of this morning to the stubborn, hurt little girl standing there now?

"What happened?" Bonnie asked Mrs. Snavely.

"She wouldn't eat her lunch," Mrs. Winters butted in, her chest puffed out in indignation, her voice cold and harsh. "She's going to learn to obey the rules or else!"

"That's all? She wouldn't eat her lunch!" Bonnie fumed.

Mrs. Snavely sighed heavily and looked at Mrs. Winters. "You've already paddled her. Isn't that enough?"

Paddled her! For not eating! Bonnie gritted her teeth to hold in her anger, but Mrs. Winters had no trouble expressing hers. "No child in my classroom gets away with disobedience.

She is going to do what I say, if I have to carry her back to my room and lock her in the closet!"

Mrs. Snavely's lips tightened. "Bonnie, please watch your sister. I want to talk privately with Mrs. Winters." Mrs. Winters had no choice but to let Paula go and follow her.

Bonnie expected Paula to run. To her relief, Paula just stood there, rooted to the floor. She couldn't hear what Mrs. Snavely and Mrs. Winters were saying, but after a few minutes, an unhappy Mrs. Winters turned and walked away.

Mrs. Snavely came and stood in front of Paula, who refused to look at her. Kindly she said, "This is your first day. I realize this is all new to you, so I'm going to give you some time. Bonnie will stay with you and whenever you are ready, I want you to go back to your class. Can you do that for me?"

To Bonnie's amazement, Paula looked up into Mrs. Snavely's compassionate eyes and nodded. Mrs. Snavely took Bonnie aside. "Give her time to calm down. If you have any more trouble, come to my office and get me." Bonnie nodded.

Paula stood in the same spot for a very long time. Finally, she walked up the stairs and down the hall. As they passed Mrs. Armstrong's second grade classroom, Paula stopped and stared through the small window in the door. After a while, Paula spoke for the first time. "She's so nice to her class." Bonnie could have cried at the longing in her voice.

A moment later, the door opened, and Mrs. Armstrong came out. "Bonnie, why aren't you two in your classes?"

Bonnie explained as best she could. Mrs. Armstrong glanced toward Mrs. Winters' classroom. A sympathetic look came over her face. She knelt down to Paula's level and said softly, "I understand. But you can't stay here all day." She held out her hand. "May I take you to your class?" Again, Paula surprised Bonnie by nodding. Mrs. Armstrong turned to Bonnie. "Go to your class. I'll take good care of her."

In spite of Mrs. Armstrong's promise, Bonnie worried all afternoon. Mrs. Winters might get revenge in the classroom.

As soon as the last bell rang, she sped to Mrs. Winters' room. The second Paula came out the door, Bonnie asked, "Are you okay?" Paula nodded, but didn't say a word.

All the way home on the bus, Paula was silent. Bonnie heard Annette asking her what was wrong. She refused to answer. Walking in the lane, Paula trudged along, not saying a word, her blond head hanging down. As they neared the house, she turned to Bonnie and said resolutely, "I made up my mind! If Mrs. Winters *ever* tries to touch me again, I'll scratch her eyes out!" And Paula meant what she said.

As soon as they entered the house, Mommy said calmly, "Bonnie, watch the boys. I want to talk to Paula alone." They were upstairs for a long time. The boys grew restless and naughty before they finally came down. Paula's face showed no emotion as she passed Bonnie on her way outside.

Mommy went to the sink and began paring potatoes for supper. "Set the table please, Bonnie," was all she said.

Bonnie blurted out, "Paula was just scared, that's all."

To her surprise, Mommy agreed. "I know. Mrs. Snavely told me that was probably the case when she called."

"Then why was Mrs. Winters so mean?"

"She believed she was right. Some teachers feel they must rule with an iron hand, or the kids won't respect them."

"But over eating lunch?" Bonnie questioned.

"I know. I wish she had shown a little mercy too," Mommy admitted. "But Paula did break the rule about eating everything on your tray."

"It's a dumb rule!" Bonnie cried out.

"It seems a bit extreme to me too," Mommy replied. "Still, Paula has to obey the rules, whether she likes them or not."

"Couldn't you call the school and ask them to put her in the other first grade class?" Bonnie pleaded.

"I'm glad you love your little sister so much," Mommy said, smiling. "The way you two go at it sometimes, I wasn't sure." Then her face turned serious. "But...I don't want to be one of those interfering parents who runs to the teacher every time some little thing happens to their child. Also, I believe God allows everything to happen for a reason. So unless she actually abuses Paula, I don't feel led to do that."

"But…"

"No 'buts'…and Bonnie, I'm going to tell you what I told Paula. Mrs. Winters may not have been right; however, as Christians, we have to forgive her."

"Forgive her!" Bonnie spat out. "No!"

"Yes!" Mommy replied with finality.

By bedtime that night, Bonnie had thought over what Mommy said and concluded she was probably right about everything as usual. Still, if Bonnie had her way, she would take Paula out of Mrs. Winters' class tomorrow!

As she said her prayers, Bonnie tried to forgive Mrs. Winters, but she could not. Her bitterness was so deeply rooted that it would take a miracle to dig it out of her heart!

In the morning, Bonnie went to her parents' room to crawl in bed with them before getting ready for school. Paula, Billy, and Tommy were already there. Mommy laughed. "There's not even room left for your big toe!"

"Well," Bonnie said, "I guess I am getting a little old for this kind of thing." It saddened her to realize it was true.

Suddenly, Paula blurted out, "I'm not going to school today!" Instantly, the happy mood disappeared. Daddy sat up in bed. "Yes, you are, young lady! And I don't want to hear another word about it! Go get dressed. In fact, it's time for everyone to get up," he said, lifting Tommy and Billy out of the bed. Reluctantly, Paula climbed out after them.

Paula didn't say much at breakfast or on the way to school. All day, Bonnie dreaded getting another call from Mrs. Snavely, but the day passed without incident. After school, Bonnie asked, "Did Mrs. Winters treat you okay?"

"I did my work and she left me alone," Paula shrugged. Bonnie smiled to herself. Good! That was the end of that.

But a few days later, during afternoon recess, she saw Daddy and Paula walk into the school! Why was Daddy here? Why was Paula with him and not in school?

Bonnie hurried to the bus stop after school and waited impatiently for Paula. As soon as she spotted her, she ran toward her, burning with curiosity. "What happened?"

"I walked home." Paula said as though it were nothing.

"What? That's at least three miles! Why did you do that?"

"Mrs. Winters said I had not done my work right and held my paper up for the whole class to see. Then she ordered me to go to the blackboard and write the alphabet. A lot of the kids have been to kindergarten, but I'm just learning the alphabet. I can't write all the letters yet, so I just walked out."

"What did Daddy do when you got home?"

"He punished me, but then he said, 'We're going back to the school, and I am going to take care of this.'"

"What happened next?" Bonnie was almost afraid to ask.

"Nothing. Daddy talked to Mrs. Winters. I don't know what he said, but she was nice to me the rest of the day."

All the way home and later, while she did her homework and chores, Bonnie wondered what Daddy had said, but as curious as she was, she didn't have the courage to ask him.

That evening, after Mommy took Billy and Tommy upstairs to bed, Daddy turned off the television just as *Ozzie and Harriet* came on. Bonnie and Paula looked at each other, puzzled and upset. The whole family loved that show!

"I want to talk to you girls," Daddy said. Seeing their worried faces, he added, "No, you're not in trouble, but in view of what happened today, there are a few things I want to be sure you both understand. First of all, the Bible teaches we should respect those in authority. So, when you're in school your mother and I expect you to obey. We will not tolerate disobedience to the rules. Is that clear?" They both nodded.

"On the other hand," Daddy went on, "as your father, I am also your protector. If someone or something is hurting you, it is my responsibility to look into the matter. Girls, in the future, please come to me if something like this happens."

Bonnie nodded. Paula crawled into Daddy's lap. He tousled her hair and went on. "Paula, I had no idea you were still having trouble. I knew it had to be something bad for you to walk home, so I decided to have a talk with your teacher."

Now was Bonnie's chance. "What did you say to her?"

Daddy laughed. "Curiosity killed the cat," but he continued, "I simply told her my daughter felt she didn't like her, and for Paula to walk all the way home there had to be something very wrong in that classroom. I did not want this to ever happen again, and I hoped she would take whatever steps were necessary to see that it didn't, so I wouldn't have to."

Bonnie's heart swelled with love for Daddy because of what he had done. She hurried over and gave him a hug.

Daddy cleared his throat and said gruffly, "Okay, now that we have that settled, let's watch the rest of the show."

Every day for several weeks, Bonnie asked Paula the same question, "How did Mrs. Winters treat you today?" Her answer remained the same, "She's being nice to me."

One day as they walked in the lane together, Paula startled Bonnie by saying, "I've forgiven Mrs. Winters."

"What? How could you after what she did to you?"

"Because the Bible says to."

"I know that, but *how* can you?" Bonnie asked again.

"I don't know. I *was* stubborn—and she's not mean to me anymore. I've been praying for her and asking God to change her heart. I guess he changed mine instead."

Suddenly, Bonnie was ashamed of herself. If Paula could forgive Mrs. Winters after the terrible time she put her through, Bonnie ought to be able to forgive her too.

That night, when Bonnie prayed for Mrs. Winters, a darkness she hadn't even known was there, lifted from her soul, and flew away. She had forgiven Mrs. Winters and it felt wonderful!

Chapter 20

AUTUMN DAYS

While Paula was having such a hard time adjusting to first grade, Bonnie was thoroughly enjoying being a sixth grader. She loved to read and used her new library privileges to good advantage, reading book after book. With the freedom she now had to leave the grounds, she hurried to the store across the street after school and bought candy or ice cream bars.

Every day, she came to know the new girl better. Yvonne was pretty with long brown hair, an oval face, and thick eyelashes. At first, she was quiet and shy, but little by little, she was opening up and their friendship was growing.

Only one thing kept Bonnie's joy from being complete. On the first day of school, notices had gone home informing parents of polio immunization shots being given in two weeks. After that, whenever it was mentioned, she cringed.

"I hate shots!" Bonnie admitted, as she stood in line when the day came, watching those ahead of her getting injections.

"I'm afraid too," Barbara admitted.

"Don't be babies!" Sheila said, but she looked scared too.

"I don't like shots either," Kathy confessed, "but it's better than getting polio."

Bonnie agreed, but that didn't ease the fear in the pit of her stomach. She let her friends go first, building up her courage. After her turn, Yvonne mouthed, "It didn't hurt much," but when Bonnie's turn came,

she trembled all over.

The nurse smiled. "It'll be over before you know it." Bonnie felt a burning pinprick. "All done!" she announced.

"See," Sheila gloated. "Nothing to it!"

Bonnie nodded, trying to look as if it had been a breeze, but she was glad it was over. There would be more shots in the future, but for now, she could relax.

When Bonnie and Paula arrived home from school that day, Mommy greeted them with some good news. "Your Aunt Anne had her baby. It's a girl! After two boys, she and your Uncle Chuck are thrilled. Her name is Cindy."

"If she had waited until tomorrow, she would have been born on baby Tommy's third birthday," Bonnie said, rather sad that it hadn't happened that way.

"Well," Mommy laughed, "I think your aunt's mighty glad the baby's here." She sighed wistfully and added, "I guess we should stop calling Tommy 'baby Tommy.' He's a big boy now...." Mommy's voice dropped off. Bonnie finished the sentence in her mind...*and there will soon be another baby.*

The next week, Daddy received a letter from his sister Eva. It contained more baby news. She was expecting her first child. It was due soon after Mommy's baby. Now, even though one baby had been born, there were again five pregnant women—Mommy and four aunts!

The last week in September, something happened to take everyone's mind off babies for a while—the new television season started. The Bedi household was more than ready for it. *I Love Lucy* was still a favorite, but Daddy also liked *The Red Skelton Show* and the police drama, *Dragnet,* while Mommy enjoyed the game shows, *The $64,000 Question* and *Beat the Clock.*

Bonnie liked Saturday morning television because there was one kids' show after another. Her favorite was *Captain Midnight*, a scary science fiction. Paula liked *Sergeant*

Preston of the Yukon, with its exciting tales of a courageous Canadian Mountie and Billy loved *The Adventures of Wild Bill Hickok*, a shoot'em-up western.

But their most favorite kids' show of all was a new one that aired every evening right after supper—*The Mickey Mouse Club*. The children who sang and danced on it were called "Mouseketeers." Bonnie's favorite was Annette Funicello. Paula liked all the girls, and Billy adored cute little Cubby O'Brien.

In early October, on Bonnie's eleventh birthday, the family waited until after *The Mickey Mouse Club* was over to eat supper. When Mommy called everyone to the table for the celebration, Billy was missing.

"Has anyone seen Billy?" Mommy questioned.

Bonnie and Paula shook their heads. Daddy cocked his. "Shhh! I hear something." They all got quiet, and sure enough, they heard it too. Thuds, along with muffled singing, were coming from inside the stairway. Daddy got up to investigate. Mommy followed, and Bonnie, Paula, and Tommy trailed behind her. Daddy opened the door, and they all squeezed onto the stairway landing.

There, in front of them, was little Billy, on his knees, climbing the stairs, banging away with his toy hammer on each step as he went up—bam…bam…bam…in rhythm to the Mickey Mouse Club theme song, which he was belting out at the top of his lungs. …*Mickey Mouse…Mickey Mouse, Forever let us hold your banner high! high! high! high! Come along and sing the song, and join the jamboree…M-I-C-K-E-Y M-O-U-S-E….* The whole family burst out laughing. Little Billy turned around, gave them an impish grin, then turned back and continued up the stairs. Not until he hammered the last step at the top would he stop singing and allow Daddy to carry him back down.

Billy's cute little escapade gave Bonnie's birthday dinner a happy start, and later as she tried on one of her gifts, a much-needed pair of dress shoes, the phone rang. When Mommy hung up, she announced, "You have another new cousin. Her name is Janice Snader." Bonnie smiled. This time the timing had been perfect! Her new cousin had been born on her birthday! Her special day was complete.

The weather grew steadily colder, and one night in mid-November, the temperature dropped below freezing. Mommy said it was time for Bonnie to move back in with Paula. Bonnie didn't like giving up her room; but she had to admit, it was much warmer snuggling up close to Paula in the cozy double bed than it had been in her lonely single bed.

A few nights later, Mommy invited all her children to crawl into bed with her for a bedtime story. Bonnie was a big girl now, but she still loved these special cozy times. When Mommy finished reading, she announced, "The baby is kicking up a storm!" then asked, "Do you want to feel it?"

A chorus of "yeses!" answered her. One by one, she took their hands and placed them on her stomach. Each face lit up as they felt the miracle of new life inside of Mommy. Suddenly, Bonnie couldn't wait for the baby to be born.

Two days after Thanksgiving, Aunt Marylou gave birth to a baby boy named Bobby, to the delight of Billy and Tommy who were glad for a boy cousin after two girls.

"Now," Mommy said, "we can relax and enjoy the Christmas season. No more babies are due until February."

Chapter 21

THE PINK DRESS

"Oh, my!" Mommy exclaimed as she helped Bonnie try on her good winter dresses. "You've grown like a weed! Nothing fits! We're going to have to get you a few new dresses, especially since you're singing in the Christmas cantata in three weeks. I'll have to scrounge up the money."

Mommy was frugal. Every piece of clothing was cared for and worn until it was threadbare or passed down to the next child. So shopping for new clothes was rare, and Bonnie was secretly glad she had grown so fast.

The following Saturday, they made a trip to Lancaster where they traipsed from store to store while Bonnie tried on dress after dress, with no success. If Mommy liked it, Bonnie didn't. If Bonnie liked it, Mommy didn't. Mommy leaned toward practical. Bonnie preferred pretty.

Finally, Mommy said, "It's getting late. Let's try Watt & Shand's. It's a little expensive, but they have nice dresses."

As they entered the clothing department, a flash of pink on one of the dress racks caught Bonnie's eye. She rushed over and pushed back the hangers to get a better look. Instantly, she fell in love with the lovely carnation-pink chiffon dress.

Mommy was not quite as happy. "It's beautiful, I'll admit," she said, "but not very serviceable."

Bonnie could not take her eyes off the dress with its scalloped collar, puffed-shoulders, sheer sleeves, trim waistline, and flared skirt with rows of frilly chiffon.

Mommy examined the price tag and shook her head. "It's too expensive."

With great reluctance, Bonnie left the heavenly cloud of pink behind, and for the next half-hour, she again tried on dresses. Several of them she rather liked, although nothing compared with the pink dress.

A sales lady noticed them and asked, "May I help you?"

Mommy explained they had found some dresses they liked, but hadn't decided which ones they wanted yet.

"Did you know we're having a special sale today? All dresses with white tags are forty percent off."

Mommy rummaged through the dresses in her cart. Her face lit up when she spied a white tag on one of them. "Bonnie, you liked this one, and it's a great deal. Now if we can just find one more that's on sale, we'll be all set."

Suddenly, Bonnie had a thought. Oh, how she hoped she was right! She turned to the sales woman and asked entreatingly, "Is that pink chiffon dress over there on sale?"

"Let me check."

Bonnie held her breath. In a few moments, she saw the sales woman returning with the dress in her hand. "It's on sale. Would you like to try it on?"

"Oh, yes! May I, Mother?"

Mommy looked doubtful, but nodded.

Bonnie slipped into the dress and Mommy zipped it up. Bonnie glanced at herself in the mirror and drew in her breath. That attractive young lady could not possibly be her!

Mommy gasped too. "You look very pretty!"

"Please Mommy, please! May I have this dress?"

Mommy sighed. "It's not very practical...but it is on sale...still it's a little too dressy...but you look so beautiful in it.... She hesitated again, and then said, "I hope I don't regret this, but, if it means so much to you, you may have the dress."

If Bonnie had not been such a big girl, she would have run over to Mommy and given her a kiss. Instead, she cried out, "Oh, thank you! You won't regret buying it. I promise!"

All the way home, Bonnie held the dress in her lap. When she modeled it for the family, they ooh'd and aah'd. Paula gushed, "I can't wait until you grow out of it, so I can wear it," and Daddy said, "My little girl is growing into a beautiful young lady." Bonnie blushed with pride. Afterward, she carefully hung the dress in her wardrobe, deciding to wait to wear it for the first time the night of the cantata.

In school a few days later, Mrs. Ehman announced the class would be performing a silent drama as their part in the last assembly before school let out for the holidays. The purpose of the skit would be to show that God is there for anyone who is willing to come to Him, no matter what race or creed, whether rich or poor, famous or unknown, prisoner or free. This would be accomplished by using scenery, which they would make, by the way the characters dressed, and by the expressions on their faces. There would be no words.

Mrs. Ehman concluded by adding, "I have seen this drama performed before and the beauty and meaning of it brought the audience to tears. We are going to practice until we can do the same thing. I'll be handing out your parts tomorrow."

After school, Bonnie went up and stood by Mrs. Ehman's desk. Seldom had she had the courage to ask a teacher for anything. Now she wanted something badly enough to try.

Mrs. Ehman smiled and asked, "Do you need something?"

"I...I..." Bonnie stammered, "I want to be the rich lady."

Mrs. Ehman appeared taken aback. "Why?"

"I just got a beautiful new dress...." Bonnie stopped. She couldn't think of how to say what she meant.

She needn't have worried. Mrs. Ehman understood. "I see. Yes, you may have the part." Bonnie practically floated out the door.

Everyone in the school was performing in the assembly and notes went home inviting the parents. Mommy was coming. Bonnie wanted to surprise her. The only thing she would tell her was that she was wearing her pink dress.

The afternoon of the assembly, after the sixth graders watched the first through fourth graders perform, they quietly left the auditorium, donned their costumes, and stood nervously waiting in line off stage while the fifth graders finished performing their part of the program. Then the auditorium lights dimmed, soft organ music began playing, and the curtains slowly opened. Bonnie heard the audience catch their breath in awe as a glowing, candle-lit church with beautiful stained glass windows appeared on stage.

Then, one by one, her classmates filed into the church: a beggar, a black man, a cripple, a judge, a prisoner.... Some knelt in prayer; some appeared sad and broken; some held their arms up in devotion; some were ragged and needy; some had faces streaked with tears; some bowed their heads in shame....

Bonnie entered last of all and stood by the altar in her fancy pink dress, a rapt expression of adoration on her face; a beautiful, wealthy woman, who in spite of her fancy clothes, recognized her need for God and had come to worship Him on Christmas Eve.

The scene remained frozen in time as the curtain slowly closed. There was dead silence for a moment, and then the audience broke out in thunderous applause.

As they hurried offstage, Mrs. Ehman praised them. "You were wonderful! I'm very proud of you."

At home, Mommy exclaimed, "It was so beautiful and meaningful, all those different types of people worshipping God! I had tears in my eyes! And the pink dress was perfect for your part. It seemed like you really *were* that pretty, rich woman!"

Although Mommy didn't realize it, she had spoken the truth. Bonnie had not been acting. From the moment she put the pink dress on; she *had been* that pretty, rich woman. And the adoration of God—well, that had been real too.

Chapter 22

NEW THINGS IN THE NEW YEAR

"New Year's Day 1956," Mommy said as they pulled into Grandpa's driveway for the Christmas get-together. "It's the perfect day to meet the newest members of the Bedi clan."

Bonnie agreed. She climbed out of the car and ran into the house. The new babies were already being passed around the room from aunt to uncle to cousin. She had to wait her turn, which was a long time in coming but when it did, it was more than worth it. She had forgotten how awesome newborns were with their soft, sweet-smelling bodies, tiny hands and feet, and kissable little faces. Holding three-month-old Cindy and one-month-old Bobby brought a yearning for their own baby. Suddenly March seemed so far away. When it was Paula's turn to hold them, Bonnie saw the same look of longing on her face. Even Billy and Tommy enjoyed cuddling the darling little babies.

Later, on the way home, the four of them began arguing over whether their baby would be a boy or a girl. The boys never cared before. Now, since holding little Bobby, they suddenly decided they wanted a boy and that Mommy should start taking the blue vitamins.

"It's too late," Paula protested. "She's been taking the pink vitamins all along. It's going to be a girl!"

"I want a baby brother," Billy declared.

"Me too!" Tommy practically worshipped his big brother and always agreed with whatever he said.

Daddy put an end to the disagreement. "We don't know whether it will be a boy or girl, but God does. He has already decided what we will have, so there's no use arguing."

Paula whispered to Bonnie, "I still want Mommy to take the pink pills. I have a plan." (Every time Mommy brought home a bottle of vitamins, Paula went through them, took out the blue ones, and put them aside for Mommy to take back to Dr. Weaver at her next appointment.) The minute they reached home that evening, Paula hurried to the cupboard, found the stash of blue pills, and hid them, to Mommy's amusement. Fortunately, for Paula, by the following morning, the boys had already forgotten all about the baby. They were too busy playing with their toys. After several days had passed and the boys didn't mention the vitamins again, Paula breathed a sigh of relief. Bonnie had to admit she did too.

A week later, on Mommy's birthday, Daddy came in the kitchen door with a big grin on his face. "I realized on the drive back from the Bedi family get-together, with all six of us crammed into our small two-door Oldsmobile, that, whether we have a boy or a girl, we need a new car before the baby arrives. So I called your Grandpa Snader to see if they had any good deals at the car lot where he works and…well…Annabell, come and see your birthday present!" He motioned for everyone to follow him outside.

Parked in the driveway was a shiny light blue four-door automobile. "It's a 1951 Buick," Daddy excitedly told Mommy, "a one-owner in good shape. What do you think?"

"It's a nice car, and we really do need it, but can we afford it?" Mommy appeared happy and worried at the same time.

"We'll manage," Daddy said. "Don't worry." He opened the front passenger door. "Climb in, Dear." Then he added, "Kids, look!" He opened one of the back doors. "You won't have to squeeze behind the seats anymore to get in."

All four of them climbed into the back seat. It was so big and roomy that they all fit, and for once, they didn't argue over who was going to sit by the doors. As they drove out the lane, Daddy started singing "Happy Birthday" to Mommy, and they all joined in. It was a wonderful, joyous ride.

Chapter 23

BARBARA'S ANNOUNCEMENT

That night it started raining. For almost a week, it rained every day, reminding Bonnie of how much she hated the cold gray days of January. Still, if you didn't consider the horrible-tasting cod liver oil Mommy insisted everyone take, the freezing cold bedrooms, and the long shivering walks in and out the lane for school, the days weren't that bad, and the evenings by the potbelly stove were quite cozy and pleasant.

There were other things to be thankful for as well. Her parents, realizing they needed to spend more time with their growing family, no longer taught the adult Sunday school classes at church. It meant Bonnie didn't have to watch the little ones while Mommy studied her lesson, and Daddy could make pancakes on Sunday mornings as he used to long ago. And his pancakes were the best—light, fluffy, and yummy!

At school, things were great too. Sheila and Kathy were in the other sixth grade class, and, being together so much, they became best friends, which worked out well because Barbara, Yvonne, and Bonnie were also becoming close. But one morning on the bus, Barbara had upsetting news.

"When school ends, my family is moving away."

"What? You can't!" Bonnie wailed in distress.

"I don't want to," Barbara said sadly, "but we are."

"I'm just getting to know you," Yvonne complained. "You can't just up and move! Oh, it's so unfair."

"I was worrying *I* might have to move. Now you're the one who is!" Bonnie shook her head in disbelief.

"We probably won't see each other again after this year" was Barbara's downhearted reply.

Later at recess, Yvonne said solemnly to Bonnie, "At least, we'll have each other." Then she brightened. "I have an idea. Let's ride our bikes to visit each other this summer."

"That's a great idea," Bonnie agreed, but her heart was heavy over losing her friend, and she hadn't even left yet.

She had a hard time keeping her spirits up that night. Mommy noticed. "Is there something bothering you?"

"Barbara's moving away after school is out."

Mommy stopped rolling pie dough, wiped her hands, and sat down at the table beside Bonnie. "I know it's hard to lose a friend, but life is all about change. Sometimes we just have to accept things and move on, even though it's hard."

Tears welled up in Bonnie's eyes. "I'll miss her so much. Things will never be the same."

"That's true, but do you know what? I think God knew this was going to happen. That's why he brought your new friend, Yvonne, into your life."

Bonnie had not thought of that. "Yvonne did say maybe we could ride our bikes to each other's homes this summer."

"See what I mean? But there is one thing I want you to keep in mind...." Mommy rose from the table and put her hand on Bonnie's shoulder, and then continued in a gentle, firm voice, "We're planning to move eventually too."

That night in bed, Bonnie thought through everything that had happened that day. On one hand, it was wonderful to know God loved her so much that He had provided a new friend for her even before she knew she was going to need one. On the other hand, it hurt dreadfully to know she was going to lose Barbara, especially since Barbara had never accepted Jesus into her heart.

The only thing Bonnie could do now was pray Barbara would come to know Jesus someday in the future. She would also pray for herself—that she never, ever had to move!

Chapter 24

PETER PAN

The week after Barbara announced her upsetting news, it again rained every day as if the weather were as sad as Bonnie was at the changes entering her life. Not only did it rain—it snowed. It was not the kind of snow where school was canceled, and everyone shouted "hallelujahs" and went sledding—it was a miserable sleety snow mixed with rain, and Bonnie and Paula still had to go to school.

The walks in and out of the lane were wretched. Cold rain dripped on them, in spite of the umbrella they shared; mud splashed up on their leggings and caked on their boots; and the cold dampness chilled them to the bone.

The only bright spot in that dreary week was watching the musical *Peter Pan*. It had aired for the first time the year before, and Bonnie and Paula, who had sat glued to the television then, were again in front of it, waiting for the show, ten minutes before it was due to come on.

At first, Bonnie was fascinated by the fact that the part of Peter Pan, a young boy, was played by a shorthaired woman. Soon, though, she was drawn into the captivating story of a boy who lives in Never Land, a place where no one ever grows up. His friends Tinkerbell, the fairy, and Wendy, a young girl, fly with him to Never Land, where they have all kinds of adventures. When Tinkerbell is poisoned and Peter tells the television audience the only way to save her is to clap if you believe in fairies, Bonnie found herself clapping loudly right along with Paula. And when Wendy decides she can't stay in Never Land but must go back home and grow up, Bonnie felt Peter's pain at the loss of his dear friend.

But the most heart-rending scene of all takes place years later when Peter comes back and finds that Wendy is an adult with a daughter of her own. When Wendy gives him permission to take her daughter Jane to visit Never Land, Peter is delighted. However, when Wendy longs to go along too, Peter says the saddest thing, "You can't. You see, Wendy, you're too grown up."

Later, as Bonnie lay in bed, listening to the raindrops splattering on the window, her mind kept going over the decision Wendy made. Bonnie was the same age as Wendy. If she had the same choice to make, what would she do?

It was comfortable and safe being a little girl with her parents taking care of her and having all the responsibility. But she was also looking forward to being in junior high next year, becoming a missionary someday and far in the future, becoming a mother and grandmother, although she couldn't imagine ever being old enough to be a grandmother!

The next day after school, Bonnie decided—though it was against the rules—to go inside the high school building, which was within walking distance of the grade school, and look around. After all, she would be a student there next year. Feeling guilty, she stepped inside and hastily walked around the bottom floor. In the middle of the school was a large auditorium and all the way around it on the outside were classrooms. It was the same upstairs, except she passed a few doors marked with their purpose, such as "Library" and "Home Ec." She wanted to explore more, but, afraid of being caught, she hurried back down the stairs and outside.

However, she had seen enough to know she wanted to experience what it would be like to be in those classrooms, what it would be like to graduate, and what it would be like to be an adult. She realized too, that in order to experience those things, she would have to accept the changes that went along with growing up.

Chapter 25

STUCK IN THE MUD

"Let's cut through the field," Paula suggested as they climbed off the school bus on the Monday after all the rain.

Bonnie glanced at the field. "It's too muddy."

"No, it isn't!" Paula snapped back.

"Yes, it is!" Bonnie retorted. "We're not going that way."

"You're not my boss!" Before Bonnie could grab hold of her, she was off. She managed to take four or five steps into the field before her boots began sinking in the mire.

"Come back!" Bonnie called after her. "You'll get stuck."

"No, I won't!" Paula yelled back and kept on going.

Bonnie hollered again, "Come back. It's too muddy."

Undeterred, Paula plodded on. The suction of the mud was so strong she could barely lift her feet. She continued on, sinking deeper with each step, until her feet were stuck like glue. Suddenly, the stubborn look disappeared from her face. She cried out, "Help me!" and began to sob.

Bonnie started across the field to rescue her, but only took a step or two before her boots sank deep into the soggy

ground. If she did not backtrack now, she too would be stuck.

Paula saw her retreating and screamed, "Don't leave me!"

"I have to go get help," Bonnie shouted back.

"Nooo! Don't leave me," Paula bawled louder.

91

"I'll get Mom!" Bonnie took off, running at top speed. She burst in the door and, catching her breath, explained to her startled mother what had happened. Instantly, Mommy grabbed her coat, took off her shoes and socks, and hurried out into the freezing weather, calling back, "Mind the boys."

Through the kitchen window, Bonnie watched her. With each step, Mommy worked hard to pull her legs up out of the mud. It took her a long time to reach Paula. In spite of being over seven months pregnant, she yanked Paula up out of her boots and half-carried, half-dragged her back to the house.

After what seemed like an eternity, they entered the lean-to shed, covered with mud and exhausted. Bonnie took them a basin of hot water. While they stripped off their mud-stained clothes and washed up, she took the stairs two at a time, grabbed two warm housecoats and rushed back down.

Mommy and Paula were shivering uncontrollably. "Thaank yoou!" Mommy said. Her teeth chattered as she donned her robe and helped Paula into hers.

Afterward, they sat in the warm kitchen, wrapped snugly in their housecoats, drinking hot chocolate. Chilled to the bone, they were still shivering when Daddy arrived home.

He asked worriedly, "Are you both okay?"

"We're fine," Mommy said. "We just need to warm up."

"What possessed you, Bonnie," Daddy asked, sounding angry, "to let your sister try to cross that muddy field?"

Bonnie didn't want to get Paula in trouble, but she didn't want to lie either. "We...we made a mistake."

"Well, from now on, you are to use the lane!"

"Yes, Daddy," both girls meekly replied, glad to get away with only a scolding.

Later in bed, Bonnie confronted Paula. "Why didn't you listen to me? You almost got us both into big trouble."

"I didn't think it was that muddy," she defended herself.

"Next time, think twice and don't do anything so foolish!"

"I won't," Paula promised.

Chapter 26

DADDY HAS A BAD WEEKEND

Paula kept her promise—for four days.

The Dyer family from church invited the Bedi family to supper on Saturday night. Mommy wanted everyone to look their best, so on Friday night, they went shopping for shoes for the boys, hair ribbons for Paula, and socks for Bonnie. When they arrived home, Daddy let everyone out of the car before backing into the garage. "Is it clear?" he called out.

Mommy looked around and answered, "Yes." Daddy still checked the Buick's rearview mirror before backing up.

All of a sudden, out of the corner of her eye, Bonnie saw Paula dart behind the car, disappearing inside the garage. A few seconds later, there was a horrendous scream. The car stopped short, halfway into the garage. Daddy jumped out and ran to the other side. Paula was sitting with her left leg bent under her and her right one stretched out in front of her by the rear tire. She was holding her ankle and writhing in pain.

Daddy stood there for a second, a look of disbelief on his face. "What happened? How did you get here?"

Between hysterical sobs, Paula said, "I slipped and fell."

Daddy turned to Mommy. "You said it was all clear!"

"It was. I don't understand...."

"My ankle hurts," Paula whined.

Daddy gently moved her ankle and she cried out. But when he had her stand up, although she winced in pain, she was able to bear her weight on it. "Thank God, it's only badly sprained. I'm surprised it isn't broken—or worse."

Mommy inspected the ground. "Look at this!" She pointed to an indentation in the dirt floor. "We've had so much rain lately, it seeped under the garage door. The ground is soft, so when the tire ran over her ankle, it gave way, saving her ankle from far worse damage. God was surely looking out for her!"

Paula spent what was left of the evening soaking her foot in ice water. She cried and fussed that it was too cold. Mommy said it had to be done to keep the swelling down.

That night, fidgeting in pain, Paula woke Bonnie up. "It hurts," she whispered.

"It's your own fault! Why did you run behind the car?"

"I was curious about how it would feel to be run over."

"You stuck your ankle under the car on purpose? How could you do such a dumb thing?" Bonnie couldn't believe it.

"I thought I'd get a lot of attention."

"Was it worth it?" Bonnie asked, knowing the answer.

"No, it hurts! Please don't tell Mommy and Daddy what I did," Paula pleaded. "I promise not to do it again."

"I've heard that before," Bonnie said sarcastically.

"Please!" Paula begged.

"Okay, but Daddy really feels bad, and Mommy thinks it's her fault, so this is your last chance. Next time, I'm telling!"

The following morning, Paula's ankle was an ugly purple. Daddy wrapped it tightly in an old, torn-up piece of sheet, and by evening, she was able to hobble to the car for the trip to the Dyers' house wearing her fancy new hair ribbons.

The rest of the family looked spiffy too. Bonnie wore her new anklets with her other new dress from Watt & Shand. Mommy looked beautiful and Daddy handsome as usual. The boys were handsome too, dressed in their Sunday best with their hair perfectly parted and smoothed back with Vaseline.

As they drove to the Dyer house, Daddy gave strict orders, "I want you to behave tonight and use your best manners."

"Yes, Daddy," they all promised. Bonnie stared hard at Paula until she mouthed, "I will!"

This time, she kept her promise. This time, it was Billy and Tommy who got themselves into trouble.

The dinner went perfectly, with everyone on his best behavior. Afterward, Bonnie and Paula played Parcheesi on the dining room table with the Dyers' teenage son Vernon. The boys played in the kitchen with a few toys Mrs. Dyer provided, and the adults went into the living room to chat.

About a half-hour later, Daddy passed through the dining room on his way to check on the boys. Bonnie heard Daddy speak, and by the tone of his voice, she knew something was wrong. Curious, she listened with one ear.

"You know better than this! That candy was not offered to you. You could have broken Mrs. Dyer's pretty glass candy jar or injured yourself standing on that chair trying to reach it. Go stand in the corner! Tommy, you in this corner. Billy, you in that corner. Don't get out until I come back!"

Daddy left and all was quiet in the kitchen. Bonnie got involved in the Parcheesi game and forgot about the boys until Daddy came back through the room to check on them.

"Oh, no!" Daddy exclaimed loudly when he entered the kitchen. Bonnie, Paula, and Vernon ran to see what had happened. Mommy and the Dyers also came running.

Daddy was standing in the middle of the kitchen with the boys, staring at the corners of the room in dismay. The boys' heads had left big permanent Vaseline grease stains on the lovely flowered wallpaper on both sides of each corner.

"My beautiful new wallpaper!" Mrs. Dyer shrieked.

Mr. Dyer made light of it. "These things happen sometimes. Luckily, the paperhangers gave me some leftover pieces. I'll call them and ask them to come and wallpaper over the spots."

"You'll do no such thing! It's my fault. I'll repair it," Daddy declared. The Dyers accepted his offer, but the evening was ruined and not long afterward, they were on their way home. Bonnie and

Paula never had a chance to finish their Parcheesi game.

At home, Mommy took Paula and the boys upstairs to bed. "I'm calling it a day too," Daddy mumbled, following them. He looked tired and upset.

Mommy came back downstairs and slumped down on the sofa beside Bonnie. It was the perfect opportunity for Bonnie to ask her about something, which had been bothering her.

"Why is Paula so stubborn sometimes?"

Mommy laughed. "You noticed that, did you?" Then she turned serious. "There are many types of personalities in this world, and we need them all. Paula is strong-willed and determined, which helps her do things most people are afraid of, but it also causes stubbornness. You're a deep thinker with a vivid imagination, but you are more fearful and have trouble being patient and forgiving." Bonnie nodded.

Mommy continued. "Billy is a born leader, but sometimes he can be a little bossy and one-track minded. Tommy's the opposite, he's a follower—easy-going and loving—but his curiosity gets him into trouble, like tonight, for instance."

"So we all have good points and bad points?"

"Well put!" Mommy praised her. "That's right. The job God has given us as Christians is to use our good features and work on controlling the bad ones. And remember," she cautioned, "it's easy to see other people's faults. What we should really be concentrating on is correcting our own."

Bonnie decided she would work on one of her bad points—impatience—and try to be more patient with Paula.

Mommy yawned. "Time for bed. It's been a long day."

"Is Daddy okay?" Bonnie blurted out, worriedly.

"It's been a rough weekend for him. He felt bad enough about running over Paula's leg and now, the grease spots on the Dyers' walls! What could possibly go wrong next?"

The following day after church, they found out. Mr. Ivan took Daddy aside and told him they would have to move off the farm.

Chapter 27

A DISMAL FEBRUARY

In the car on the way home from church, Daddy gave Mommy the bad news.

"I can't believe Ivan would do such a thing!" Mommy said, sounding as though she were going to cry. "You have always bent over backward trying to help him. How could he hire someone else? How does he expect us to find another place to live in only two months?" Mommy ranted on. "And in the dead of winter! With me expecting a baby...."

Bonnie could not believe it either. They were going to have to move! No more riding the tractor or walking to the meadow. No more feeding the steers or gathering the eggs. No more riding down the barn hill or climbing through the hay tunnels. No more sleeping on the balcony or meditating in her secret hideout. And no more anniversary celebrations.

Then she had another horrible thought. Not only would she have to leave the farm, but she might have to go to a different school! She would never see her friends again!

When she told her friends at school, they were as upset as she was. Yvonne was the most distressed of all. "First Barbara and now you! We've just become friends. Now you're both going to leave," she grumbled. "It's so unfair!"

Billy and Tommy were too young to realize what was happening, but Paula was quite unhappy about leaving too. "I like it here. I'm not going!" she decided stubbornly.

"Sorry, Sweetie. You don't have a choice," Mommy told her gently. "None of us do." Although Mommy had never been happy on the farm and was the only one who wanted to move, she was not happy they had to leave right now. She often worried aloud, "Where are we going to find a house? How are we going to make the car payments now that we'll have to pay rent? How am I going to get ready to move when I'm so exhausted from being big and pregnant and taking care of the four kids I already have?" Then, she would read her Bible and pray, and murmur, "God will provide."

Daddy minded it most of all. He had loved farming ever since he was a little boy helping on his father's farm. Though he had to work elsewhere to provide for his growing family, he was a farmer at heart. Then too, he had never been fired before, and he took it personally, feeling as if he had somehow failed to do his best. On top of that, he too worried about where they would find a house they could afford and how he was going to pay all the bills without the extra money he made helping on the farm.

Daddy's birthday, Billy's fifth birthday, and Valentine's Day passed by without much celebrating while Daddy searched for a house, but found nothing. The weather outside the farmhouse was cold and rainy, and the atmosphere inside was not much better. Mommy was big and uncomfortable from her pregnancy, Daddy was preoccupied with all the problems of meeting his family's needs, and Bonnie and Paula were upset about moving. Only the boys played happily, unaware of the drama going on around them.

One Sunday afternoon, Mommy decided to visit her sister Josephine. "Her baby is due next week. It's the only chance I'll get to talk to her before then." Whenever Mommy felt down, she always visited Aunt Josephine.

The minute they entered Aunt Josephine's house, Mommy perked up. Even Daddy and Uncle Bob chuckled when the two women compared their big bellies. Although Mommy had a month to go, and Aunt Josephine was due anytime, Mommy's tummy was bigger. "I always have big babies, and they're always two weeks late," Mommy stated wryly.

Instead of playing with her siblings and three younger boy cousins in the basement, Bonnie decided to read a book in the dining room where she could hear the women talking. She had found out you could learn a lot by eavesdropping on adults when they didn't think you were listening.

First, the women caught up on all the news on their large family. Bonnie was surprised to hear Mommy say, "Did you know Lois is expecting? The babies just keep coming!"

"Yes, she called me yesterday. I'm so happy for her," Aunt Josie said, "especially since her last baby boy only lived one day. This will help heal the hurt. We need to pray our sister's pregnancy goes well and she has a healthy baby."

Mommy agreed and then went on to tell Aunt Josephine all about having to leave the farm and being unable to find a house. "The best thing we can do is pray," said Aunt Josie. And that's what they did, right there and then.

Afterward, Mommy sounded happier as they began discussing the names they had picked out for their babies. "Do you mind if we name our baby Billy too, if it's a boy?" Aunt Josie asked.

"Not at all," Mommy gave her permission. Then she said, "If ours is a boy, we're going to name him Joseph after Bill's dad, and if it's a girl, I've chosen the name Phyllis. Bill likes that name too, but we disagree on the middle name. I want Elizabeth. He wants Elaine." Bonnie had not known that.

On the way home, she brought up the subject. "I like the name Mommy picked for our new baby— Phyllis Elizabeth."

Billy objected. "It's going to be a boy and have a boy's name."

"A boy's name," Tommy repeated.

"If it's a boy, its name will be Joseph Scott," Daddy informed them all, "and if it's a girl, it will be Phyllis Elaine."

"A boy named Joseph Scott," Billy declared.

Paula disagreed. "It's going to be a girl, and her name is going to be Phyllis Elaine."

"It's going to be a boy, Joseph Scott," Billy countered.

"A boy, Joseph Scott," Tommy repeated.

"I like Phyllis Elizabeth," Bonnie added her two cents.

"No, Phyllis Elaine!" Paula said emphatically.

Daddy laughed. "There's no use arguing about it until we see if the baby is a boy or a girl." Bonnie was glad to hear him laugh. Talking to Uncle Bob had cheered him up too.

But he didn't stay cheery for long. Every day he watched the paper for a house to rent, but there was not one house listed big enough for their family. When Aunt Josie had a baby boy two weeks later and named him Billy, Daddy was still looking, and it was almost the end of February. There was only one month left until they had to move.

Daddy was frantic to find a house and Mommy was praying fervently God would provide one. But since Bonnie had heard the news they had to leave the farm, she had been very mad at God. She had prayed and prayed He would keep them on the farm, and she couldn't understand how He could possibly say "no." She moped around feeling sorry for herself most of the time. When Mommy pleaded with her to pray about finding a house, she refused. She didn't want a new house! And what was the use of praying? God just said "no" anyway.

On the last day of February, the telephone rang. When Daddy hung up, he smiled for the first time in a while.

"The old Hollinger house just up the street is going up for public auction in ten days. That was Mr. Graver from the church. He thinks I might have a chance of getting it fairly cheap. It has a large downstairs and four bedrooms upstairs, but no running water and needs lots of fixing up."

Daddy was happy. Bonnie was not! She remembered that dark, ugly, spooky house from years ago when she had gone there Halloweening. She hated that eerie old house!

Chapter 28

LONESOME FOR YOU, ANNABELL

For the next ten days, there was nothing to do but wait. Mommy prayed God would give them the house. Bonnie hoped He wouldn't. Maybe if they had nowhere else to go, Ivan would be forced to allow them to stay on the farm.

Mommy also prayed about where the money was going to come from. One night, out of the blue, she cried out, "Why didn't I think of it before? If we cash in the insurance policies we have on the kids, it might cover the down payment!"

Daddy hurried to his desk, pulled out the policies, and did some figuring. "By golly, Annabell, you're right! I think it will be just enough! Now, if only I can outbid everyone else, without the house costing more than we can afford...."

"God is able," Mommy said earnestly, but the waiting was hard. To keep from worrying, she declared, "I'm going to begin packing. Bonnie, bring the boxes down from the attic. We'll sort through them." Unhappy about packing for a move she didn't want, Bonnie headed for the attic, grabbed two boxes, carried them down and went back up for more.

On top of the next box was a pack of letters held together by a blue ribbon. Curious, Bonnie untied the ribbon, opened the first one, and began reading, "My dearest Annabell...." Who would be addressing Mommy in such a way? She turned the letter over. It ended with, "All my love, Bill."

Bonnie suddenly realized she had found love letters from Daddy to Mommy. Without thinking, she began reading. In clear, bold handwriting, Daddy wrote to Mommy telling her how pretty her brown eyes were, how lovely her dark hair was, and how beautiful she looked to him. Then, in passionate words, he expressed his love for her, said he missed her terribly, and wanted to marry her. At the bottom of the letter was a P.S. which read, "Lonesome for you, Annabell."

Shocked and feeling somewhat guilty, as though she had entered a forbidden place, Bonnie quickly put the letter back, retied the ribbon, and carried the box downstairs.

Immediately, Mommy noticed the ribbon had been retied. "Did you open these?" she asked, sounding displeased.

"I read one," Bonnie admitted.

Mommy looked perturbed. "Please don't read anymore."

"I won't, Mommy," Bonnie said, relieved that she was not in trouble, "but tell me, how did you meet Daddy?"

Mommy hesitated for a moment, then said, "Go get the rest of the boxes and while we sort them, I'll tell you."

Fifteen minutes later, as the younger children played in the living room and Daddy watched the evening news, Mommy told Bonnie a simple, yet charming, love story.

"It all started when my next-to-oldest sister Pauline and her family moved to Cedar Lane, a village about an hour from here. Not long after they moved, Pauline's husband became sick and could not work. Pauline had to get a job in order to pay the bills. My dad asked me to take off from high school and baby-sit for them. I was in my senior year and didn't want to do it. He said I was being selfish and should think about my sister and her needs. I left a few days later."

"Is that why you never finished school?" Bonnie asked.

"Yes. But though I regret it, I would do it again to help my sister and to find a wonderful man like your daddy!"

She continued on, "Pauline rode to work with a neighbor man named Walter Fessler."

Bonnie interrupted again, "You mean Uncle Walter?"

"Yes, only at the time, I hadn't met him or his wife, your Aunt Jen, or her brother Bill, your daddy."

"It sounds so strange for you to say you didn't know Daddy," Bonnie interjected.

"It seems unbelievable to me now too," Mommy said, chuckling. Finishing a box, she set it aside and started another one. "Anyway, a few weeks before I arrived, Bill came to stay with the Fesslers while he worked at a farm nearby. He was only supposed to be there a week or so while he waited to enlist in the Army. But things changed."

"What happened?" Bonnie asked, as she rose to put a few items of clothing that Mommy had discarded into the ragbag.

"World War II was going on. Most young men had already been drafted into the Army, and the farmer Bill worked for was desperate for help. When he discovered how hard-working Bill was, he went to the draft board and pleaded for a deferment, so Bill could continue working for him. It came through one day before your daddy was to leave."

Bonnie stopped sorting her box, shocked at what she just found out. "If Daddy had not gotten a deferment, he would have left for the Army, and you two would never have met!"

"Isn't it amazing how God works?"

Dazed, Bonnie nodded, and Mommy continued. "One morning after that, I accompanied Pauline to Walter's house to catch her ride. Bill was also leaving for work and Walter introduced us." Mommy smiled as she thought back on it. "Immediately, I was attracted to him, and I could tell he liked me, but we were both too bashful to do anything about it."

"How did you get together then?"

"The Fesslers, Pauline, and I attended a cottage prayer meeting. One night, Bill and his cousin came too. His cousin passed me a note during the service asking me out. I was not attracted to him. I wrote back 'no.' Afterward, he came to me and said, 'If you won't date me, will you go out with my cousin Bill?' From talking to Pauline, I knew Bill had graduated from high school as president of his class, was well mannered, and didn't drink or swear. And I had not failed to notice his twinkling blue eyes, tan muscular arms, and trim handsome build. I didn't have to think twice! I said, 'yes.' A few minutes later, Bill came over and asked me out."

Mommy stopped. "Tell me more!" Bonnie pleaded.

"After that, we spent every moment we could together. On one date, your dad pulled me two miles in a wagon to a restaurant that served good oyster soup! Other times, we just sat on Pauline's porch listening to music, stargazing, and talking. It wasn't long before we were madly in love and wanted to get married, but my parents said I was too young."

"What happened next?"

"Something dreadful! Your Aunt Pauline and her family moved back to Manheim. Of course, I had to go along."

"Did you miss Daddy?" Bonnie quizzed.

"We missed each other like crazy! That's when your daddy wrote all those love letters to me, adding "Lonesome for you, Annabell" as a P.S. to every one of them."

"Why did he do that?"

"It was a popular country song back then. Whenever we heard it on the radio, your daddy would sing along with it, saying the words to me. So, when I actually moved away, the song became our song because he missed me so much."

"Did you go back to visit him?" Bonnie wanted to know.

"Actually, he came to me. Every Friday night, he rode the trolley up to Lancaster, took a bus to Manheim, and stayed at Pauline's for the weekend, then rode back on Sunday night. It wasn't enough. We begged our parents again to let us get married, and, this time, to our great joy, they said 'yes.' We didn't have any money, so your Aunt Esther, my oldest sister, out of the goodness of her heart, gave us a nice wedding. And the rest is history."

Bonnie hugged her mother. "And I'm sure glad it is!"

Chapter 29

AMAZING GRACE

The day before the auction, Daddy received a call from a nearby farmer. He invited Daddy to farm tobacco on the halves. He would provide the land and Daddy would supply the labor. When the crop sold, they would divide the profit.

Daddy was ecstatic. "Tobacco is a good money crop. The extra money I make should be enough to see us through!"

Mommy had never liked farming tobacco because it was used to make cigars and cigarettes, but although her lips tightened, she only said, "It does seem providential, Bill."

"Now I have the income we'll need, and the down payment is covered," Daddy said, "if only I can win the bid!"

"I'll be praying the whole time," Mommy promised. But the next morning, she woke up feeling sick. The baby was already overdue, and she was huge, achy, and miserable.

"Go to bed, Annabell," Daddy ordered. "Take the kids up with you. Bonnie, help your mother." He hurried out into the cold morning. Bonnie could see the anxiety on his face.

Mommy went to bed, but instead of resting, she began giving orders. "Paula, you're in charge of entertaining the boys. Bring some toys up for them. Bonnie, go get my record player. Plug it in by the table over there and put on the "Amazing Grace" record." She lay back, looking exhausted.

Soon the words and music of "Amazing Grace" filled the room. It was a much slower version of the song than Bonnie had ever heard before. The singer drew out every word. *A...A...maa...zi...ing...graaace...howww...sweeet...*

As the song played slowly through, Bonnie watched Mommy's face. Her eyes were closed and her lips were moving in silent prayer. As the song ended, Mommy said, "Play it again, Bonnie, and as you listen, pray with me. Pray hard that we get the house."

Bonnie put the record on again and Mommy closed her eyes, but Bonnie would not. She didn't want that ugly house! She sat there, stone-faced and unyielding, throughout the long, drawn-out song.

When it finished, Mommy said, "Play it again." Bonnie couldn't believe it, but she did as she was told. This time tears streamed down Mommy's face as she prayed.

When the song finally finished, Mommy said the same thing. "Play it again." Instead, Bonnie asked a question.

"Why does that house mean so much to you?"

Mommy wiped her eyes with the end of the sheet, took a deep breath, and patted the bed beside her. "To explain, I'll have to continue the story about when I met your daddy."

"I want to hear it," Bonnie said, glad for the distraction.

"Okay, here goes. As soon as your daddy and I were married, we moved into a little rental house near the farm where he worked. We had only been married a short time when I found out I was pregnant with you. As you know, I always get very sick with my pregnancies. On top of that, your daddy hurt his back and could no longer work on the farm. We had no money and neither of us could work. My sister Pauline was kind enough to offer to let us move in with her, so we moved to Manheim. I babysat her boys and in a few months, your daddy was better and found a good job at the asbestos company. Then, before I could even finish the pretty nursery I was preparing for you, you were born."

Mommy gave her a hug before going on. "When you were only a few months old, your daddy was called up to the Army again since he no longer worked on the farm. We were devastated at the thought of being apart. I remember standing on the train platform that morning with you in my arms, waving good-bye, sadly wondering how long it would be until I saw him again. Late that evening, there was a knock on the door and there stood Bill! He had been rejected because of a suspicious-looking mole on his back. You never saw such a happy couple! He was told to return in three months, but by then, the war was over, and they were no longer accepting men with children."

"Do you think that was God?" Bonnie questioned.

"I know it was!" Mommy said emphatically, before continuing. "When you were six months old, we were finally able to rent our own place. It wasn't much. It had one room up and one room down with a steep stairway connecting them, which you managed to fall down, giving us the scare of our lives." Again, Mommy gave her a hug before going on.

"About this time, we met a very nice family who adored you and was willing to baby-sit, so I got a job at the silk mill. For the next three years, I saved every penny I earned because we had a dream. We wanted to buy a house of our very own."

"One day, however, Bill found out about this farmhouse. He could work on the farm in the mornings and work second shift at the asbestos factory, bringing in more income, so I could stay home with you. For the plan to work, we needed a car and some decent furniture. The only money we had was what we had saved. It was very hard for me to give up my dream, especially when the bank told us we almost had enough money saved for a down payment on a house."

"Why did you give it up then?" Bonnie wondered.

Mommy sighed. "First of all, although the Hornburgers, who babysat you, were wonderful people, I felt guilty about not being home with you. Then too, I thought a farm would be a good environment for you to grow up in."

"You were right!" Bonnie couldn't help saying.

"Yes, I was," Mommy agreed. "But the biggest reason was because of your daddy. He missed farming terribly. How could I keep him from doing something he loved so much?"

"Then why don't you stay here?" Bonnie pleaded.

"Because we don't *have* a choice. But, even if we did, this farm belongs to Ivan. It will never be ours. Your daddy is a machinist now, not a farmer, and he has accepted that. And Bonnie, try as I might for your daddy's sake, I have never been happy here. I hate the flies, the smell of manure, and all the hard work it takes to make someone else successful. But, most of all, my dream of a home of our own has never died. I feel the Hollinger house is God's answer to my prayers."

Bonnie rose from the bed and put the record on again. As it droned on, the words "amazing grace" sank deep into her soul. Mommy believed in those words, so much so that she was staking her future on them. For the first time, Bonnie let herself accept the fact they were going to leave her beloved farm. In her heart, she knew Daddy didn't want to leave either. He was doing it because it was the right thing to do. If Daddy could be so unselfish, maybe she could be too.

Downstairs a door slammed. Bonnie heard Daddy take the stair steps two at a time before he burst into the room, his face beaming, and announced, "We got it, Annabell. We got it!"

Mommy gave a cry, jumped out of bed, and flew to him, hugging him as if she would never let go. "Thank God! Oh, thank God! Oh, Bill! We have a house! We have a house!"

When Daddy had a chance to breathe, he added, "It was the most amazing thing! All the local farmers wanted the house because of its valuable land and were bidding against each other, but when they figured out I was bidding for it, they stopped bidding and let me have it!"

It was then, after hearing how God had softened the hearts of those uncompromising, business-minded farmers that Bonnie's own heart finally melted, and she admitted to herself what she had not been willing to accept before—the Hollinger house was God's will for her and her family.

Then she had a cheering thought. *It won't be so bad. I'll be going to the same school, and I can walk the short distance from that house to this farm anytime I want.*

Chapter 30

A NEW BABY

The next day at church, Mommy and Daddy told everyone the news. Mr. Graver, who had told them about the house, could not believe how well the sale had gone. Others were amazed the house had sold for only $6,400! A few, who knew they struggled financially, wondered aloud how they could even afford a house. When Mommy told them how perfectly God worked out the money for the down payment, they were astounded at God's "amazing grace" as Mommy called it.

It was a day of rejoicing and thanking God. Mommy made a special lunch to celebrate. A feeling of immense relief, great joy, and hope for the future permeated the whole house.

But when the sun rose Monday morning, they still faced problems: they only had a short time to get ready to move; the baby was coming; and Mommy was worn out. Then too, the down payment for the house was due in two days, but the money from the insurance policies would take a month to clear. God had come through for them. Now they must take the next step—swallow their pride and reach out for help.

"I've thought about the down payment all day," Daddy said that evening. "I think Ivan would loan us the $1,300."

"No!" Mommy rose from the kitchen table, yelling at Daddy. "We are *not* going to him after he put us out!"

"Now, Annabell," Daddy said soothingly, "Ivan has been good to us over the years, and he has a point. I haven't been putting in the hours I used to. He has to think of his own interests. Besides, he's the only one I know who *can* help us."

Mommy frowned, but when she answered Daddy, she was calmer. "It's humiliating, but do what you think is best."

After Daddy left for the Snyders', Mommy stood up and said to Bonnie, "I've been doing some thinking of my own. I helped my sister Lillian out when Debbie was born. Maybe she'll return the favor. I'll give her a call right now."

Before Daddy returned, everything had been worked out. Lillian, her husband Fred, and their thirteen-month-old daughter would come and stay with them until they moved.

The instant Daddy returned, Bonnie knew he had been successful. He was grinning from ear to ear, and in his hand was a check. Mommy couldn't help but smile. Her frown reappeared, however, when she learned Ivan was charging interest. "The loan's only for a month, for Pete's sake!"

"I'm thankful he helped," Daddy said. Mommy nodded, but her face showed she was not too happy with Mr. Ivan.

The following evening, while a light snow fell, the Wiegand family moved their bed, a crib, clothing, and a few other belongings into the two unused rooms at the back of the farmhouse. And not a minute too soon. It snowed all night into the next day, and the farm was completely snowed in.

Mommy worried that if her labor started, a helicopter would have to transport her, but fortunately, the baby waited.

The next morning, the sky was clear and the roads were plowed. Daddy and Uncle Fred shoveled the lane. As Daddy left to take Bonnie and Paula to the bus stop and then go to work, Mommy said to him, "Stay near a phone!"

A worried look passed over Daddy's face. "They're calling for another big snowstorm, worse than this one, in about twenty-four hours. Call me at the least little sign."

In the car, Bonnie begged to stay home. Daddy shook his head. "Your aunt will take care of things. Don't worry."

When Bonnie and Paula arrived home from school that afternoon, Aunt Lillian met them at the door. "Your mom's started labor. Your parents are at the hospital; they didn't want to take a chance of being snowed in. It will probably be a while till we hear from them." She was right. At bedtime, they still had not heard a thing, but Aunt Lillian made them go to bed. "You have school tomorrow. Say your prayers and go to sleep. You'll know if it's a boy or a girl by morning."

"I know it's going to be a girl," Paula said and drifted off to sleep. Bonnie couldn't sleep. She was old enough to know having a baby wasn't easy, and she kept thinking of the baby her Aunt Lois had lost. She prayed for Mommy and the baby.

The next thing she heard was Daddy's voice calling, "Hey you sleepy heads! Don't you want to hear about the baby?" It was daylight! Bonnie grabbed her housecoat and went thundering down the stairs with Paula and the boys.

Daddy, Aunt Lillian, and Uncle Fred were at the kitchen table having coffee. In front of Daddy were a pink vitamin and a blue vitamin. Teasingly, he moved his hand back and forth above them while they all held their breath. Then his hand scooped down and picked up the pink one.

Bonnie and Paula let out hoots of joy. "I told you so!" Paula gloated. Billy groaned. "Another girl." Tommy tried to copy him, but his groan sounded so funny that Aunt Lillian started laughing and couldn't stop. Her laugh was contagious. Soon everyone was laughing. It was a very happy breakfast.

Then Daddy went to bed to catch up on sleep, and Bonnie and Paula went to school where they told everyone about their new baby sister. As they were riding the bus home from school, it began to snow. By the time supper was over, it had become a blinding blizzard. Daddy couldn't go to see Mommy and the baby, but he said he didn't mind. He was just glad Mommy had the baby before the blizzard came!

The next morning, Daddy and Uncle Fred had to shovel the lane again before Daddy could go to the hospital. It snowed more the next two days, but with chains on his tires, he managed to get to the hospital and back. Finally, it cleared up, and Daddy brought Mommy and the baby home.

They all took turns holding baby Phyllis. When Paula held her, her face shone with love. When the boys held her, they decided a girl wasn't so bad after all. When it was Bonnie's turn, she couldn't believe she had ever questioned whether she wanted another baby—she was so adorable. As she kissed the sweet little face, she remembered to ask, "What did you decide about her middle name? Is it Elizabeth or Elaine?"

"Your mother cheated on that one," Daddy said, trying to look upset. "They brought in the birth certificate on the day I was snowed in. Since I wasn't there to put in my two cents, she wrote in 'Elizabeth.' By the time I found out, it was too late." He smiled at Mommy. "I guess Elizabeth is better. After all, it's the name of a queen."

The following days were spent getting to know the little "queen," as well as enjoying their baby cousin Debbie, and frantically packing to move. Mommy was supposed to be resting, but with so much to do, she often disobeyed Dr. Weaver, to Daddy's concern. "You'll have a setback."

"I'm fine," she insisted. "We'll never be ready to move in time with all the work! Lillian can't do it all, and Fred works." Daddy didn't say anything. He knew it was true.

Ten days after baby Phyllis was born, Aunt Eva's husband called and said they had just had a son, Avin Duane Duncan. "Well, that's the last of this batch of babies," Mommy said, "but your Aunt Lois has already started the next batch. Who knows how many cousins you kids are going to have before it's all said and done!" *A lot!* Bonnie said to herself.

The days flew by, and most of the time, Bonnie was too busy to think much about the move. But sometimes at night, she thought about never sleeping in her room again, and the tears flowed. And once or twice, she was sure she saw tears in Paula's eyes. Daddy never said a word, but grinned and joked as he helped pack in the evenings. But, from time to time, he stared out the window with a faraway longing in his eyes.

Chapter 31

MOVING DAY

The last day of March dawned cold but clear.

"Thank goodness," Mommy said. "We've had such a miserable winter. At least we'll be able to move in decent weather." She yawned as she served a quick breakfast of cereal and milk. She had stayed up late doing last-minute packing with Aunt Lillian, and Bonnie had heard baby Phyllis crying several times during the night.

As soon as breakfast was over, Mommy began giving orders. "My brothers Sammy and Sonny will be here to help in an hour. We need to be ready. Bonnie, clear the table, do the dishes, and then pack them! Paula, you're in charge of keeping an eye on the baby and the boys! Call me if you need me. Lillian and I are going up to strip the beds." Daddy headed to the barn to do his morning chores for the last time.

In an hour, they were all finished with their assignments, but Mommy's brothers were running late with the moving truck. Standing on the cold porch with nothing to do but wait was depressing. Even Mommy looked sad, now that their final day on the farm had actually come.

Suddenly, Daddy yelled, "Who wants me to ride a pig?"

Squeals of delight and "yeses" rang out. Uncle Fred said, "I can't wait to see this!" and Aunt Lillian laughed.

Mommy wasn't sure. "There's so much work to do...."

"It's the last time I'll ever be able to do it," Daddy reminded her. She smiled then and said, "All right."

Everyone ran to the barnyard and climbed up on the fence. Daddy entered and picked the fattest pig. Before the pig knew what was happening, he jumped on its back. Instantly, the pig went wild. It took off, squealing and running, with Daddy hanging onto its neck for dear life. It was the most comical sight Bonnie had ever seen! When Daddy fell off, right into a pile of manure, peals of laughter rang out.

Daddy didn't quit. He got up and ran after the pig. Now the pig was determined not to be caught. Daddy had to chase it all over the barnyard before he was able to mount it again, just to be thrown off a few seconds later, like a rodeo rider. Again and again, he chased the pig, jumped on it, rode it a few seconds, and then was bucked off. Finally, tired and grinning, he gave up to taunts and hoots of laughter from everyone, including Mommy's brothers who had arrived just in time to enjoy the show. Bonnie's sides hurt from laughing.

"You stink!" Mommy said as Daddy teasingly tried to hug her.

"I cheered everyone up, didn't I?" Daddy called back, grinning as he headed for the shed to change and wash up.

Then Bonnie understood. They had to move, but they didn't have to be gloomy. Daddy had taken care of that!

Everyone helped move, but it still took the better part of the day. The family of seven moving out had a lot more "stuff" than the little family of three that had moved in years ago. It was fascinating to watch the furniture from the second floor being handed down over the balcony railing, but Bonnie Paula, and the boys had to stay clear because of the danger. However, they were allowed to take turns riding the moving truck back and forth to their new home just up the street.

At the new house, Bonnie helped carry boxes inside. The house was as bad as she had pictured it. The wallpaper was yellowed, the paint was peeling, and the air smelled musty and stale. There was not even a sink in the kitchen, only a pump outside. And she already hated the outhouse!

Daddy saw her dismay. "Don't worry, Little Bird. I'll fix up this old house so nice you won't recognize it!" He gave her a squeeze and hurried off. When Daddy made a promise, he kept it. Bonnie's spirits lifted. Maybe someday, though she didn't think it was possible, she'd come to love this rundown, old-fashioned house as much as she loved the farmhouse.

Finally, after many trips, the last piece of furniture from the farmhouse was loaded, along with the picnic table and the yard swing. The men and boys headed out to set things up at the new house. Bonnie, Mommy, Aunt Lillian, and Paula cleaned the old one. Mommy didn't want the people who moved in after them to think she was a sloppy housekeeper.

When the house was spotless, they walked through it one last time. Memories of the last eight years flooded Bonnie's mind and tears stung her eyes. Paula looked sad too. As Mommy locked the door, she said one last time, "Be it ever so humble, there's no place like home."

As they drove out the lane, Bonnie looked back at the farm where she had lived for as long as she could remember. In that old farmhouse, a family had loved and cried, worked and played, struggled and grew. And it had housed them securely as they did. She would never forget the little farm down the lane.

Then she turned around in her seat and faced the future.

Does Bonnie ever adjust to her new home? Can she stand up to peer pressure during her teenage years? Will she ever become a missionary? Be sure to read Book VIII and find out!

To contact author – kbsiegrist@ij.net

CPSIA information can be obtained at www.ICGtesting.com
Printed in the USA
LVOW060823261011

252063LV00002B/1/P